Best Easy Day Hikes
San Francisco's East Bay

D1007688

Help Us Keep This Guide Up to Date

Every effort has been made by the authors and editors to make this guide as accurate and useful as possible. However, many things can change after a guide is published—trails are rerouted, regulations change, facilities come under new management, etc.

We would love to hear from you concerning your experiences with this guide and how you feel it could be improved and kept up to date. While we may not be able to respond to all comments and suggestions, we'll take them to heart and we'll also make certain to share them with the authors. Please send your comments and suggestions to the following address:

The Globe Pequot Press
Reader Response/Editorial Department
P.O. Box 480
Guilford, CT 06437

Or you may e-mail us at:

editorial@GlobePequot.com

Thanks for your input, and happy trails!

FALCONGUIDES®

Best Easy Day Hikes Series

Best Easy Day Hikes
San Francisco's East Bay

Tracy Salcedo-Chourré

FALCONGUIDES®

GUILFORD, CONNECTICUT
HELENA, MONTANA

FALCONGUIDES®

To buy books in quantity for corporate use
or incentives, call **(800) 962–0973**
or e-mail **premiums@GlobePequot.com.**

Copyright © 2009 by Morris Book
Publishing, LLC

ALL RIGHTS RESERVED. No part of this
book may be reproduced or transmitted
in any form by any means, electronic or
mechanical, including photocopying and
recording, or by any information storage
and retrieval system, except as may
be expressly permitted in writing from
the publisher. Requests for permission
should be addressed to The Globe
Pequot Press, Attn: Rights and Permis-
sions Department, P.O. Box 480, Guilford, CT 06437.

Falcon and FalconGuides are registered
trademarks and Outfit Your Mind is a trade-
mark of Morris Book Publishing, LLC.

Maps created by Ryan Mitchell ©2009 Morris
Book Publishing, LLC

Library of Congress Cataloging-in-Publication
Data is available on file.

ISBN: 978-0-7627-5104-4

Printed in the United States of America
10 9 8 7 6 5 4 3 2 1

Contents

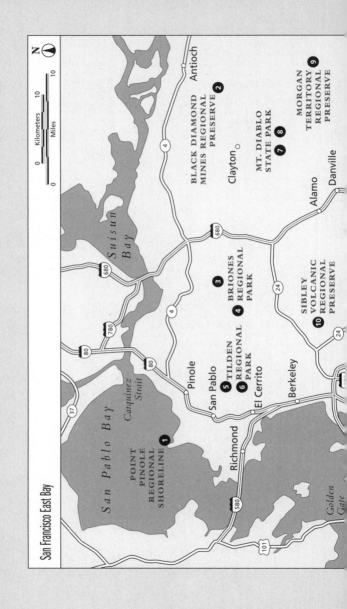

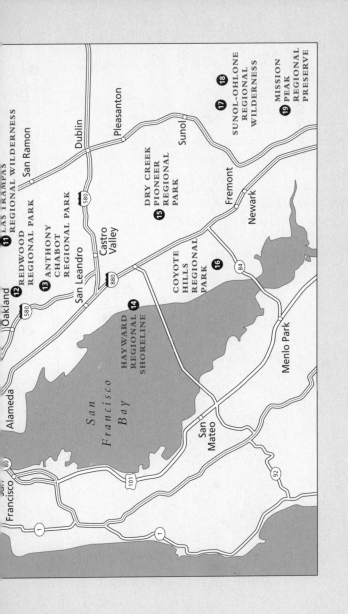

Acknowledgments

I am indebted to the many hikers and lovers of wildlands who have worked over the years to preserve parks and trails throughout the Bay Area. A guidebook like this wouldn't be possible without their efforts.

Thanks to the land managers who have taken the time to review the hikes described in this guide, and to guidebook authors who have shared their impressions of and experiences on San Francisco area trails both in books and online. They include Shelly Lewis, David Zuckerman, Denise Defreese, Paul Ferreira, Ed Leong, Janet Gomes, and Roger Epperson of the East Bay Regional Park District.

Thanks to The Globe Pequot Press and its fine editors and production staff for inviting me to take on this project and helping me make it the best it can be.

Thanks also to family, friends, and neighbors who either introduced me to Bay Area trails over the years or offered suggestions for this guide, including the Chourré clan, my parents Jesse and Judy Salcedo, brother Nick and his wife Nancy, brother Chris and his partner Angela Jones, and many others.

My husband, Martin, and sons Jesse, Cruz, and Penn, have been unfailing supporters of my work as a writer and teacher. I'm grateful and very lucky to share my journey with them.

Map Legend

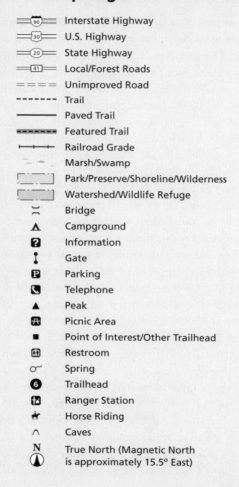

90	Interstate Highway
30	U.S. Highway
20	State Highway
41	Local/Forest Roads
= = = =	Unimproved Road
- - - - - - -	Trail
————	Paved Trail
▬▬▬▬▬	Featured Trail
⊢—⊣—⊢	Railroad Grade
	Marsh/Swamp
	Park/Preserve/Shoreline/Wilderness
	Watershed/Wildlife Refuge
≍	Bridge
▲	Campground
❓	Information
⬩	Gate
🅿	Parking
☏	Telephone
▲	Peak
🛆	Picnic Area
■	Point of Interest/Other Trailhead
🏻	Restroom
⟋	Spring
6	Trailhead
🏠	Ranger Station
🏇	Horse Riding
∧	Caves
N ⬇	True North (Magnetic North is approximately 15.5° East)

Introduction

Born in San Francisco and raised in Marin County, I grew up in one of the most dynamic metropolitan areas on the planet. The Bay Area's cuisine, music, museums, universities, theaters, freethinking population—they've combined to shape my worldview. But most profoundly, I grew up surrounded by incredible natural beauty. The landscapes of my young life included deep dark redwood groves, sandy beaches and rocky shorelines, the smell of bay laurel on hot summer afternoons, waves of golden grasses, and bright fields of lupines and poppies stretched over rolling hills. I've been very lucky.

The gift of guidebook writing was given to me by a publisher and friend in Colorado. He knew I loved the landscapes there—probably because I spent so much time gazing out the office window at the snowy summit slopes of Mount Evans—so he asked me to start writing about them. I spent years writing guidebooks to Colorado's mountain trails before my husband and I returned home to raise our children in the North Bay.

Is it any wonder, then, that I'd write guidebooks about the hills and beaches and forests that inspired me in the first place?

In the course of researching this book, I've revisited a few trails I know well, but discovered many new ones. Each recommends itself in a unique fashion, whether for its ecology, history, topography, or natural beauty. From the top of Mount Diablo to the marshes of the Coyote Hills, I hope you'll find these hikes as eye-opening and satisfying as I have.

The Nature of the Bay

Residents of the San Francisco Bay Area are almost universally outdoorsy. In the East Bay interests range from the relatively easy, like gardening, to relatively radical, like rock climbing in the Sunol-Ohlone Regional Wilderness.

Hiking strikes a middle ground, and this guide aims for that, showcasing relatively short routes that take trekkers into parks that protect redwood groves and bayside marshes, coastal mountaintops and ridges, oak woodlands and former ranches.

Wherever you wander, knowing a few details about the nature of the East Bay will enhance your explorations.

Weather

The San Francisco Bay Area essentially has two seasons, dry and rainy. The rainy season generally runs from November through March and includes rainstorms that can drop anywhere from a trace to several inches of rain. In the dry season, from April through October, very little rain falls, though fog can roll in off the Pacific at any time.

The East Bay encompasses two microclimates, bayside and inland. On the west side of the Berkeley and Oakland hills, along the Interstate 880 corridor, the effects of the ocean are more strongly felt. Temperatures are generally moderate, with daytime temperatures in winter in the 50s and 60s, and summer temperatures in the 70s and 80s. Fog is more likely to linger along the bay.

Temperatures farther inland, on the Interstate 680 corridor, are generally higher in summer, and can dip lower in winter. Average daytime temperatures in winter range from the 50s to the high 60s, but the mercury can dip to freezing during cold snaps. Inland peaks like Mount Diablo receive occasional snowfall as well. Summertime temperatures range from the 70s to the 90s, with the occasional heat wave shooting the mercury above 100 degrees. These are generally short-lived, as the bay's natural air conditioner—the fog—inevitably creeps back in.

Critters

Most likely you'll encounter only benign, sweet creatures on these trails, such as deer, squirrels, rabbits, and a variety of songbirds and shorebirds.

But the East Bay's parklands are also habitat for mountain lions and rattlesnakes. Signs at trailheads warn hikers if these animals might be present. Encounters are infrequent, but you should familiarize yourself with the proper behavior should you run across either a dangerous snake or cat. Snakes generally only strike if they are threatened. Keep your distance and they will keep theirs. If you come across a cat, make yourself as big as possible and do not run. If you don't act like or look like prey, you stand a good chance of not being attacked.

Be Prepared

It would be tough to find a safer place for a hike than in the East Bay. Still, hikers should be prepared, whether they are out for a short stroll in Tilden's botanical garden or headed to the summit of Mount Diablo. Some specific advice:

- Know the basics of first aid, including how to treat bleeding, bites and stings, and fractures, strains, or sprains. Pack a first-aid kit on each excursion.

- Be prepared for both heat and cold by dressing in layers.

- Carry a backpack in which you can store extra clothing, ample drinking water and food, and whatever goodies, like guidebooks, cameras, and binoculars, you might want.

- Some trails have good cell phone coverage. Bring your device, but make sure you've turned it off or got it on the vibrate setting while hiking. Nothing like a "wake the dead"–loud ring to startle every creature, including fellow hikers.

- Keep children under careful watch. Children should carry a plastic whistle; if they become lost, they should stay in one place and blow the whistle to summon help.

Zero Impact

Trails in the East Bay are heavily used year-round. We, as trail users and advocates, must be especially vigilant to make sure our passing leaves no lasting mark. Here are some basic guidelines for preserving trails in the region:

- Pack out all your own trash, including biodegradable items like orange peels. You might also pack out garbage left by less considerate hikers.

- Don't approach or feed any wild creatures—the ground squirrel eyeing your snack food is best able to survive if it remains self-reliant.

- Don't pick wildflowers or gather rocks, antlers, feathers, and other treasures along the trail. Removing these items will only take away from the next hiker's back-country experience.

- Avoid damaging trailside soils and plants by remaining on the established route. This is also a good rule of thumb for avoiding poison oak and stinging nettle, common trailside irritants.

- Don't cut switchbacks, which can promote erosion.
- Be courteous by not making loud noises while hiking.
- Many of these trails are multi-use, which means you'll share them with other hikers, trail runners, mountain bikers, and equestrians. Familiarize yourself with the proper trail etiquette, yielding the trail when appropriate.
- Use outhouses at trailheads or along the trail.

East Bay Boundaries and Corridors

The East Bay encompasses cities, towns, and open spaces in Alameda and Contra Costa Counties. Two major transportation corridors run through the area. The Interstate 80/880 corridor runs north-south through Berkeley, Oakland, Hayward, and Fremont. Farther inland, the I-680 corridor runs north-south through Concord, Walnut Creek, Danville, San Ramon, Pleasanton, and cities between. Interstate 580 bridges the two corridors via the Castro Valley, stretching from San Leandro on the west to Dublin on the east.

Land Management

The following government organizations and departments manage most of the public lands described in this guide and can provide further information on these hikes and other trails in their service areas.

- California State Parks, Department of Parks and Recreation, 416 9th Street, Sacramento, CA 95814; P.O. Box 942896, Sacramento, CA 94296; (800) 777-0369 or (916) 653-6995; www.parks.ca.gov; info@parks.ca.gov. A complete listing of state parks, including those in the Bay Area, is available on the Web site, along with park brochures and maps.

- East Bay Regional Park District, 2950 Peralta Oaks Court/P.O. Box 5381, Oakland, CA 94605; (888) EBPARKS; www.ebparks.org. This guide is heavily weighted with hikes that are on regional parkland for good reason: The agency has done a spectacular job of preserving open spaces from the shores of Suisun Bay south to Mission Peak, and from the wetlands of Coyote Hills east to the rangelands of Morgan Territory and beyond. Some of the parks link to wildlands preserved by city and county open space departments.

- East Bay Municipal Utilities District, Oakland Administration Center, 375 11th Street, Oakland, CA 94607; (866) 40-EBMUD (866-403-2683) ; www.ebmud.com. The mailing address is P.O. Box 24055, Oakland, CA 94623. EBMUD maintains 80 miles of trails in its watersheds. While these trails are not detailed in this guide, many of the routes herein link with them. You must purchase a permit to access the trails, which can be done online through the Web site. Call (925) 254-3778 or (510) 287-0459 for more information.

A number of regional trails span the East Bay, including the San Francisco Bay Trail (baytrail.abag.ca.gov), which follows the bay shore, and the Bay Area Ridge Trail (www.ridgetrail.org), which cruises ridgetops. Portions of the regional trails are incorporated into shorter regional paths, such as the Ohlone Trail in Berkeley and trails in Tilden, Redwood, and Chabot regional parks.

In addition, an expanding trail network links cities, public lands, schools, and businesses within the I-680 corridor from Martinez south to Pleasanton. These trails include the Iron Horse Trail, the Lafayette-Moraga Trail, the Contra Costa Canal Trail, and others. Visit the East Bay Regional Park District Web site at www.ebparks.org for more information about these routes.

Public Transportation

A number of bus, rail, and ferry services link communities in the San Francisco Bay Area. For general public transit information and links to specific transit sites, visit 511.org, or call 511 from anywhere in the San Francisco metropolitan area.

AC Transit offers bus service in Alameda and Contra Costa Counties. Route information can be accessed through the toll-free 511 system, or you can visit the Web site at www.actransit.org. Call (510) 891-4700 for more information.

The County Connection provides transit services to central Contra Costa County communities including Martinez, Walnut Creek, Danville, San Ramon, Lafayette, and Moraga. County Connection offices are at 2477 Arnold Industrial Way, Concord, CA 94520; (925) 676-1976; www.cccta.org.

Information about Bay Area Rapid Transit (BART) trains can be accessed by visiting the Web site at www.bart .gov. Phone numbers vary depending on the area of service, and are listed on the Web site. The customer information number is (510) 464-7134. The customer service address is P.O. Box 12688, Oakland, CA 94604-2688.

Bay Area ferries serving the region include the Blue and Gold Fleet and East Bay Ferries. Information for the Blue and Gold Fleet is at www.blueandgoldfleet.com; call (415) 705-8200 for more information.

Information for East Bay Ferries is at www.eastbayferry .com; call (510) 749-4972. Alameda's Harbor Bay Ferry, the southernmost East Bay ferry, can be reached by calling (510) 769-5500.

How to Use This Book

This guide is designed to be simple and easy to use. Each hike is described with a map and summary information that delivers the trail's vital statistics including distance, difficulty, fees and permits, park hours, canine compatibility, and trail contacts. Directions to the trailhead are also provided, along with a general description of what you'll see along the way. A detailed route finder (Miles and Directions) sets forth mileages between significant landmarks along the trail.

Hike Selection

This guide describes trails that are accessible to every hiker, whether a visitor from out of town or someone lucky enough to live in the East Bay. The hikes are no longer than 5 miles round-trip, and some are considerably shorter. They range in difficulty from short flat excursions perfect for a family outing to ascents up some of the region's most visible peaks and ridges. While these trails are among the best, keep in mind that nearby trails, often in the same park, wilderness, or preserve, may offer longer or shorter options better suited to your needs.

The East Bay Regional Park District alone maintains nearly 100,000 acres of open spaces in Contra Costa and Alameda Counties. These parks, along with city, county, and state parks, traverse the ridges of the Berkeley and Oakland hills, dot the shores of San Francisco Bay, and stretch inland toward the Central Valley. I've attempted to space hikes throughout the region, so that wherever your starting point, you'll find a great easy day hike nearby.

Difficulty Ratings

These are all easy hikes, but easy is a relative term. Some would argue that no hike involving any kind of climbing is easy, but in the Bay Area, hills are a fact of life. To aid in the selection of a hike that suits particular needs and abilities, they are rated easy, moderate, and more challenging. Bear in mind that even the more challenging hikes can be made easy by hiking within your limits and taking rests when you need them.

- **Easy** hikes are generally short and flat, taking no longer than an hour to complete.

- **Moderate** hikes involve increased distance and relatively gentle changes in elevation, and will take one to two hours to complete.

- **More challenging** hikes feature some steep stretches and generally take longer than two hours to complete.

These are completely subjective ratings—keep in mind that what you think is easy is entirely dependent on your level of fitness and the adequacy of your gear (primarily shoes). If you are hiking with a group, you should select a hike with a rating that's appropriate for the least fit and prepared in your party.

Approximate hiking times are based on the assumption that on flat ground, most walkers average two miles per hour. Adjust that rate by the steepness of the terrain and your level of fitness (subtract time if you're an aerobic animal and add time if you're hiking with kids), and you have a ballpark hiking duration. Be sure to add more time if you plan to picnic or take part in other activities like birdwatching or photography along the trail.

Trail Finder

Best Hikes for Coast Lovers

1 Bay View Trail Loop (Point Pinole Regional Shoreline)
16 Bayview Trail (Coyote Hills Regional Park)

Best Hikes for Children

6 Tilden Regional Park Botanic Garden
8 Rock City (Mount Diablo State Park)
12 Stream Trail (Redwood Regional Park)

Best Hikes for Dogs

3 Alhambra Creek Trail (Briones Regional Park)
9 Volvon/Blue Oak Trail Loop (Morgan Territory Regional Preserve)

Best Hikes for Peak Baggers

4 Old Briones Road (Briones Regional Park)
11 Rocky Ridge Loop (Las Trampas Regional Wilderness)
19 Hidden Valley/Peak Meadow Trail Loop (Mission Peak Regional Preserve)

Best Hikes for Great Views

4 Old Briones Road (Briones Regional Park)
7 Mary Bowerman Trail (Mount Diablo State Park)
11 Rocky Ridge Loop (Las Trampas Regional Wilderness)
19 Hidden Valley/Peak Meadow Trail Loop (Mission Peak Regional Preserve)

Best Hikes for Nature Lovers

1 Bay View Trail Loop (Point Pinole Regional Shoreline)

It's tempting to call this an explosive hike, given that the Bay View Trail and Point Pinole Trail wander through the former dynamite works of the Giant Powder Company. Instead, the hike is a peaceful affair, perfect for bird-watchers and hikers alike.

Distance: 3.4-mile loop.

Approximate hiking time: 1.5 hours.

Difficulty: Easy.

Trail surface: Gravel road, paved road.

Best season: Year-round, though winter storms may leave large puddles in their wakes.

Other trail users: Runners, cyclists.

Canine compatibility: Leashed dogs permitted.

Fees and permits: Fees are levied when the entrance kiosk is staffed. Entry is $3 per car. The dog permit fee is $2.

Schedule: The park is open from 5:00 a.m. to 10:00 p.m. unless otherwise posted.

Maps: USGS Mare Island; East Bay Regional Park District map and brochure to Point Pinole Regional Shoreline.

Trail contact: East Bay Regional Park District (EBRPD), 2950 Peralta Oaks Court/P.O. Box 5381, Oakland, CA 94605-0381; (888) EBPARKS; www.ebparks.org.

Special considerations: None.

Other: A shuttle runs every hour from 7:30 a.m. to 3:00 p.m. (Thursday to Monday) between the park entrance and the picnic areas and fishing pier. Shuttle fees are $1 for adults (12 to 61) and 50 cents for children (6 to 11). Seniors ride free. Fishing is permitted off the pier at the end of the point and along the shoreline. Please obey California Fish and Game regulations, posted on the pier. Those fishing from shore must carry a valid fishing license.

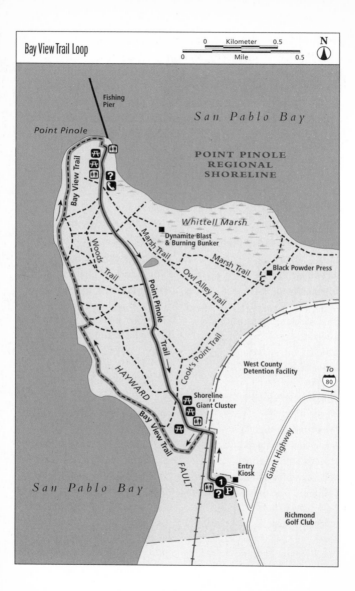

Bay View Trail Loop

0 ——— Kilometer ——— 0.5
0 ——— Mile ——— 0.5

N

San Pablo Bay

POINT PINOLE
REGIONAL
SHORELINE

Fishing
Pier

Point Pinole

Bay View Trail

Whittell Marsh

Dynamite Blast
& Burning Bunker

Marsh Trail

Marsh Trail

Black Powder Press

Woods
Trail

Owl Alley Trail

Point Pinole Trail

Cook's Point Trail

West County
Detention Facility

To
80

HAYWARD

Shoreline
Giant Cluster

Giant Highway

Bay View Trail

Entry
Kiosk

1
P

FAULT

San Pablo Bay

Richmond
Golf Club

Finding the trailhead: Point Pinole Regional Shoreline is at 5551 Giant Highway in Richmond. From Interstate 80, take the Richmond Parkway exit. Follow the Richmond Parkway southwest to Atlas Road. Turn right (west) on Atlas Road, and go 0.6 mile to Giant Highway. Turn left (south) on Giant Highway for 0.5 mile to the park entrance on the right (west). *DeLorme Northern California Atlas & Gazetteer:* Page 94 D2 and Page 104 A2. GPS: N37 59.475' W122 21.351'.

The Hike

Wandering along the edge of San Pablo Bay, with shore-birds wheeling on the sea breeze, it would be difficult to envision Point Pinole as the site of a dynamite factory.

Yet it was on this point that the Giant Powder Company churned out explosives in a thriving enterprise that, according to the park brochure, included a company town, railroad, production facilities, and a dance hall. For eighty years, the brochure explains, "[two] billion tons of dynamite were manufactured here."

Ka-boom.

These days dynamite is a distant memory, with the point instead drawing bird-watchers, picnickers, hikers, and anglers. A scenic pier juts into the bay at the end of the point, and a maze of trails slices through the eucalyptus forests and earthworks erected to buffer explosions.

Begin the hike by taking the paved Point Pinole Trail north from the trailhead, past restrooms and an information panel to a bridge that spans the Union Pacific railroad tracks. The east end of the Bay View Trail is on the other side of the tracks.

Turn left (south) on the Bay View Trail, descending through eucalyptus to the sparkling bay, then turning sharply right (northwest) to trace the shoreline. As you head northwest on the route, views open of Mount Tamalpais and Sonoma Mountain. The trail is mostly exposed, littered with wildflowers in spring and sparsely shaded by gnarly old eucalyptus.

At the 1-mile mark, a beach access trail marks a detour in the Bay View Trail, which is blocked by a huge fallen tree. Switchback up and right, climbing to an intersection where you'll turn left (northwest), rejoining the Bay View Trail.

A series of intersections in the eucalyptus woodland follows: first the Biazzi Trail on the right, then the Nitro Trail, then the Angel Buggy Trail and an unnamed trail. Stay left (northwest) on the obvious Bay View Trail. At the 1.5-mile mark you'll pass the remnants of an old packhouse and the trail that borrows its name.

Pass another series of side trails as you approach the tip of the point at 1.8 miles. The trail arcs above land's end, offering great views across the bay, then drops to a picnic area and fishing pier with equally wonderful views. A shadow pier, little more than waterlogged timbers, dates back to the dynamite days.

The return route follows the paved Point Pinole Trail, which leads southeast out of the picnic area and rolls through meadowland bordered by walls of eucalyptus to the Cook's Point Trail junction, where you'll find a complete recreation area with a sand volleyball pit, barbecues, group picnic areas, a tot lot, a horseshoe pit, restrooms, broad lawns, and views of Mount Tamalpais.

A quick downhill stretch returns you to the railroad bridge, then down to the trailhead.

Miles and Directions

0.0 Start.

0.2 Cross the railroad bridge and reach the Bay View Trail.

0.5 Pass the unsigned Cook's Point Trail at 0.5 mile; continue straight on the Bay View Trail past old eucalyptus trees, a brown-sand crescent of beach, and protected wetlands.

1.0 Reach the Bay View Trail detour. A quick jog uphill leads to where the trail resumes. The trail continues past intersections with the Biazzi Trail, the Nitro Trail, and the Angel Buggy Trail.

1.5 Reach the Packhouse Trail. The timbers and foundation of the packhouse are on the right (north). Continue straight (west) on the Bay View Trail.

1.8 Curve around the end of the point.

2.0 Reach the fishing pier and picnic area. Pick up the Point Pinole Trail back toward the trailhead. Pass the Owl Alley Trail on the left, the first of several intersections. Remain on the paved route.

2.3 Pass the China Cove Trail intersection. At the bottom of a swale, pass a side trail that leads to a freshwater pond on the left (northwest).

2.7 Pass the Giant Station Trail, continuing inland on Point Pinole Trail.

3.0 Arrive at the Cook's Point Trail intersection and the recreation area. Continue on the Point Pinole Trail.

3.4 Cross the railroad bridge and return to the trailhead and parking area.

2 Rose Hill Cemetery and Lower Chaparral Loop (Black Diamond Mines Regional Preserve)

A duo of trails in this former coal-mining district lead hikers to a historic cemetery and among the dark shafts that yielded black diamonds to the miners who worked them. Views of Suisun Bay and a walk on smooth sandstone punctuate the trails.

Distance: 2.2 miles.
Approximate hiking time: 3 hours for both trails; 1.5 hours for Rose Hill Cemetery and 1.5 hours for Lower Chaparral Loop.
Difficulty: Moderate due to steep pitches along both the Nortonville and Lower Chaparral trails. Lower Chaparral also features a stretch of smooth sandstone that requires care and concentration.
Trail surface: Paved road and dirt road to Rose Hill Cemetery; paved and gravel roads, dirt singletrack, and sandstone on Lower Chaparral Loop.
Best season: Year-round. Trails may be muddy after winter rains, and hot summertime temperatures may restrict comfortable

hiking to morning and evening hours.
Other trail users: Cyclists, equestrians.
Canine compatibility: Leashed dogs permitted where posted, in parking lots, and in picnic areas. Dogs may be off-leash on trails outside these areas provided they are kept under control.
Fees and permits: Entry is $5 per vehicle. The dog fee is $2. Mine tours are $3.
Schedule: Park hours change seasonally, and are posted at the entrance. In summer, the park is open from 8:00 a.m. to 8:00 p.m. Call the park at (925) 575-2620 or visit www.ebparks.org for current hours.

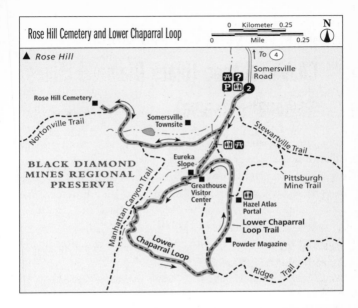

Rose Hill Cemetery and Lower Chaparral Loop

0   Kilometer   0.25
0   Mile   0.25

N

▲ *Rose Hill*

↑ To ④
Somersville
Road

Rose Hill Cemetery

Nortonville Trail

Somersville
Townsite

Stewartville Trail

BLACK DIAMOND
MINES REGIONAL
PRESERVE

Eureka
Slope

Greathouse
Visitor
Center

Pittsburgh
Mine Trail

Hazel Atlas
Portal

Manhattan Canyon Trail

Lower
Chaparral Loop

Lower Chaparral
Loop Trail

Powder Magazine

Ridge Trail

Maps: USGS Antioch South; East Bay Regional Park District map and brochure to Black Diamond Mines Regional Preserve.

Trail contact: East Bay Regional Park District, 2950 Peralta Oaks Court/P.O. Box 5381, Oakland, CA 94605-0381; (800) EBPARKS; www.ebparks.org.

Special considerations: Remain on trails to avoid contact with poison oak.

Other: Historic artifacts in Black Diamond Mines Regional Preserve are protected and should be left in place for future park visitors to enjoy.

Finding the trailhead: The park is at 5175 Somersville Road in Antioch. From Highway 4, take the Somersville Road exit. Head right (south) on Somersville Road for 2.4 miles to the Black Diamond Mines Regional Preserve boundary. Continue another mile to the upper parking lot and trailhead, where you'll find picnic tables, trashcans, and restrooms. *DeLorme Northern California Atlas & Gazetteer:* Page 105 A6. GPS: N37 57.544' W121 51.800'.

The Hike

The riches gleaned these days from Black Diamond Mines Regional Preserve include nuggets of history and snapshots of an engaging landscape. But in bygone times these steep hills and canyons yielded fortunes to miners carving black diamonds—coal—from the earth.

These two trails showcase some of the shafts from which miners extracted their livelihoods, and the cemetery that documents the deaths of workers and families who were pioneers in the foothills of Diablo.

Begin on the paved Nortonville Trail, which leads into what was once the largest coal-mining district in California. Five townsites, which supported twelve working coal mines, are scattered within the preserve's boundaries; sand for glass making was also taken from these hills. The trail offers access to the park's visitor center, the portal of the Hazel Atlas shaft, and Rose Hill Cemetery.

At the top of a rise, you'll pass an interpretive sign that overlooks the site of Somersville on the right (west) and the trail to the Stewartville Townsite on the left (east). Just beyond a large pile of tailings—the debris left after valuable ore has been removed from its source—marks a trail intersection. Here you have a choice: You can head up to Rose Hill Cemetery, then to the mineshafts along the Lower Chaparral Loop, or vice versa. The trek is described beginning with the climb to Rose Hill Cemetery, then with the journey around the Chaparral loop.

The Nortonville Trail, a dirt road that leads up to the cemetery and beyond, is a straightforward and steady climb peppered with some steep pitches. The side trail to the cemetery is at the 0.6-mile mark; turn right (northwest) on the narrow track, heading up toward the unlikely spires of cypress trees that mark the site.

Wandering among the gravestones in the cemetery is poignant and provocative. Markers for beloved matriarchs, the victims of epidemics, natives of South Wales, and a disheartening number of infants cascade down the hillside. Take the time to read some of the engravings, like this one for two-year-old Julia Etta:

Too sweet a flower to bloom on Earth
She is gone to bloom in Heaven.

The Nortonville Trail continues steeply up to the Nortonville Townsite, but to tour the mines return as you came to the Hazel Atlas trail intersection at the tailings pile. Go right (south) into a picnic area where the trail splits. You can round the Lower Chaparral Trail in either direction; for this hike, turn right (southwest) to the Greathouse Visitor Center, which was once the entry to the sand mine.

A staircase leads up to the Eureka Slope, a great gated shaft that dives into the earth. For more than thirty years in the late nineteenth century, 150,000 tons of coal were hauled out of the Eureka mine on counterbalancing railroad cars.

The Chaparral Trail climbs switchbacks from the shaft through a gnarly manzanita forest to the Lower Chaparral Loop junction. Go left (east) on the Lower Chaparral Loop, climbing first through more manzanita, then over smooth sandstone. At 1.7 miles the loop turns sharply north and drops over more sandstone past the cool cave of the powder magazine to the Hazel Atlas portal, where mine tours are offered to those who pay a small fee. From the Hazel Atlas it's a quick descent on a wide track back to the picnic area, and from there to the parking lot and trailhead.

Miles and Directions

0.0   Start.

0.2   Follow the paved Nortonville Trail past the Stewartville Trail intersection and the Somersville interpretive sign. A large tailings pile marks the intersection of the Nortonville Trail and the trail to the Hazel Atlas Portal. Go right (west) on the Nortonville Trail toward Rose Hill Cemetery.

0.3   Pass the first intersection with the Manhattan Canyon Trail on the left (south) and stay straight (up) on the Nortonville Trail.

0.5   Pass the second Manhattan Canyon Trail intersection and again remain on the broad Nortonville Trail.

0.6   Reach the side trail to Rose Hill Cemetery. The cemetery gate is less than 0.1 mile up and ahead. Explore the cemetery, then return as you came to the Hazel Atlas trailhead near the tailings pile.

1.3   Arrive back at the Hazel Atlas trail intersection and turn right (south) on the Chaparral Trail. The trail splits in the picnic area, where you'll find trashcans, tables, restrooms, and water. Go right (southwest) on the Chaparral Trail, past the Greathouse Visitor Center.

1.4   Climb the staircase to the Eureka Slope portal. Go right (west) to the Chaparral Trail, climbing a singletrack that switchbacks up the hillside behind the Eureka shaft.

1.5   Reach the Lower Chaparral Loop junction. Go left (east) on Lower Chaparral Loop.

1.7   Climb through scrub to a traverse that offers views east of Suisun Bay, then steeply up over smooth sandstone and past an airshaft on the right to a second intersection with the Chaparral Trail. Go sharply left (downhill and north) on the Lower Chaparral Loop.

1.8 The trail descends steeply over a sandstone apron—there is no distinct path, but the footing is good. At the base of the apron two paths diverge; stay right on the steeper track to a trail marker for the Lower Chaparral Loop. A quick jog to the right takes you to the powder magazine.

1.9 Drop on the sandstone track, staying left on the main path on another shaft to a garage and the portal to the Hazel Atlas mine. Railroad tracks lead out of the mine to a platform overlook in the shade.

2.0 Descend from the mine on a gravel road to the picnic area.

2.2 Retrace your route from the picnic area to the trailhead and parking lot.

3 Alhambra Creek Trail (Briones Regional Park)

The landscape is lovely, with open meadows bordering on a stream shaded by oaks and bay laurels. The views are great, across the hills to the north bay and delta. But it's the companionship of the dogs—and the dog lovers who walk them—that sets this trail apart.

Distance: 2.4-mile loop.
Approximate hiking time: 1.5 hours.
Difficulty: Moderate due to some steep slopes.
Trail surface: Dirt road, dirt singletrack.
Best season: Spring and fall.
Other trail users: Cyclists, equestrians, trail runners.
Canine compatibility: Leashed dogs permitted in developed areas of the park; dogs may run off-leash in undeveloped areas.
Fees and permits: Fees are charged only when the entry kiosk is staffed. Entry fee is $3 per car; there is a $2 dog fee.
Schedule: The park opens at 8:00 a.m. daily. Specific closing hours are posted at the entry kiosk. A curfew is imposed between 10:00 p.m. and 5:00

a.m.
Maps: USGS Briones Valley and Walnut Creek; East Bay Regional Park District brochure and map available at the trailhead and at www.ebparks.org.
Trail contact: East Bay Regional Park District, 2950 Peralta Oaks Court/P.O. Box 5381, Oakland, CA 94605-0381; (888) EBPARKS; www.ebparks.org.
Special considerations: This is dog country. They run free on the trails and free through the meadows. If you aren't up for sharing the trail with four-legged friends, you should consider another option. The park is home to rattlesnakes and mountain lions. While an encounter is unlikely, caution and common sense are advised. Rattlesnakes also pose a danger to dogs. If you allow

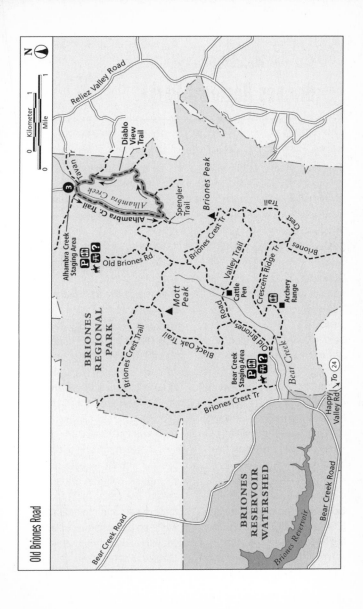

Old Briones Road

N

0   Kilometer   1
0   Mile   1

Reliez Valley Road

Diablo View Trail

Alhambra Creek

Lavan Tr

Alhambra Cr Trail

Spengler Trail

Briones Peak

Alhambra Creek Staging Area

Old Briones Rd

P

Briones Crest Tr

Valley Trail

Cattle Pen

Crescent Ridge Tr

Briones Crest Trail

Archery Range

BRIONES REGIONAL PARK

Mott Peak

Black Oak Trail

Old Briones Road

Bear Creek Staging Area

P

Briones Crest Tr

BRIONES RESERVOIR WATERSHED

Briones Reservoir

Bear Creek

Happy Valley Rd

To 24

Bear Creek Road

Bear Creek Road

yours to run off-leash, be aware that they risk a bite. Park staff reports a dog is bitten nearly every year.

Other: There are few facilities at the trailhead other than parking and an information sign. A restroom and drinking fountain are available at the picnic area adjacent to the intersection of the Alhambra Creek Trail and the Orchard Trail.

Finding the trailhead: From Highway 4 in Martinez, take the Alhambra Avenue exit. Head south on Alhambra Avenue for 0.8 mile to Alhambra Valley Road and turn right (south). Follow Alhambra Valley Road for 1.2 miles to Reliez Valley Road and turn left (southeast). Go 0.5 mile on Reliez Valley Road to the signed access road for the Alhambra Creek Staging Area. Turn right (south) on the access road and follow it to the parking area and trailhead. *DeLorme Northern California Atlas and Gazetteer:* Page 105 A4. GPS: N37 57.383' W122 07.415'.

The Hike

This pocket of the expansive Briones Regional Park—which encompasses more than 6,000 acres—features some of the most bucolic hiking in the East Bay. The loop couples an easy saunter alongside Alhambra Creek with a more challenging climb onto the Diablo View Trail. Vistas of Mount Diablo are framed in the boughs of oaks that grow on the ridgetop.

Once part of an enormous rancho belonging to the Briones family, cattle still graze on the grassy hills of the Alhambra Valley. But cows aren't the only animals that run here. On cool weekend mornings hikers let the dogs out, and they rule the trail. It's a joyous scene, full of tail wagging and sniffing, with happy masters and their families sharing in the frivolity.

The trail begins at the gate on the south end of the parking lot. The two ends of the loop meet right at the trailhead; you can hike either direction, but the route is described here in a counterclockwise direction, beginning with the Alhambra Creek Trail and ending on the Diablo View Trail.

The former ranch road that serves as the base for the Alhambra Creek Trail is wedged between the creek, which flows in winter, spring, and early summer, and a broad meadow that brims with wildflowers in season. Dogs and people have worn social trails throughout the meadowland, but the trail proper is unmistakable. A singletrack trail runs along the creek on the opposite (east) bank, offering the potential for a loop if you chose to forego the Diablo View climb.

That climb begins at the first formal trail intersection, where the Alhambra Creek Trail ends on the Spengler Trail. You'll enter cattle country as you ascend the ridge, with the grass long and free flowing on one side of the fence and cropped close to the ground on the other. Close all gates behind you as you proceed.

The Diablo View Trail meets the Spengler Trail near the top of the ridge, and true to its name, the track offers great views of the mountain to the southeast, as well as across the hills to the waters of Suisun Bay and the Carquinez Strait. All these are filtered through the gauzy canopy of spreading oaks scattered across the slopes.

The trail rollercoasters across the ridge, though the trend is generally downward. Some of the pitches are steep, but footing on the ranch road is solid. The final stretch of the loop drops through grassland to meet up with a gravel ranch road—the views here stretch 270 degrees from Mount Diablo north and west into the Alhambra Creek drainage. The staging area is visible below; drop on the gravel road to the trailhead gate and parking area.

Miles and Directions

0.0 Start just inside the gate, taking the Alhambra Creek Trail to the right (south). You'll return on the Diablo View Trail, which takes off to the left (southeast). About 100 yards from the trailhead the Alhambra Creek Trail meets the Orchard Trail. A picnic area (with water and restrooms) is on the right (north). Stay straight on the broad dirt Alhambra Creek Trail.

0.3 Social trails lead left to a watering trough for cattle and limber dogs. Stay straight (south) on the obvious Alhambra Creek Trail.

0.7 At an informal trail junction stay right (south and up) on the Alhambra Creek Trail. The trail to the left (south and down) parallels the high road alongside the creek for about 0.1 mile before climbing to meet the formal route again.

0.9 Arrive at the intersection with the Spengler Trail. The social singletrack on the opposite creek bank also ends here, offering the option for a shady return along the stream. Otherwise, turn left (east) on the Spengler Trail, which climbs out of the creek drainage.

1.1 Pass a cattle gate; close this behind you.

1.2 Pass through cropped pastureland to the Diablo View Trail junction. Turn left (northeast) on the Diablo View Trail.

1.7 Continue straight (north) on the signed Diablo View Trail, which passes a trail intersection and through another gate.

2.0 Reach a gravel ranch road and go right (north), descending past the Hidden Pond Trail intersection on the right (east). The drop is not for the weak-kneed; by contrast, a hike up this section of trail would be a great workout.

2.3 Pass the Tavan Trail on the right (north).

2.4 Arrive at the trailhead gate and parking area.

4 Old Briones Road (Briones Regional Park)

The old ranch road that links the Bear Creek watershed on the west to Alhambra Creek on the east leads to the crest of the Briones ridge and wonderful vistas.

Distance: 3.3 miles out and back.

Approximate hiking time: 1.5 hours.

Difficulty: More challenging, due to distance and a short but steady climb to the Briones ridge.

Trail surface: Dirt ranch road, a small section of pavement.

Best season: Spring and fall.

Other trail users: Cyclists, equestrians, bird-watchers, the occasional ranch vehicle.

Canine compatibility: Leashed dogs permitted in developed areas around the trailhead. In undeveloped areas dogs may run off-leash.

Fees and permits: Fees are charged only when the entry kiosk is staffed. Entry fee is $3 per car; there is a $2 dog fee.

Schedule: The park opens at 8:00 a.m. daily. Specific closing hours are posted at the entry kiosk. A curfew is imposed between 10:00 p.m. and 5:00 a.m.

Maps: USGS Briones Valley; East Bay Regional Park District brochure and map available at the trailhead and at www.ebparks.org.

Trail contact: East Bay Regional Park District, 2950 Peralta Oaks Court/P.O. Box 5381, Oakland, CA 94605-0381; (888) EBPARKS; www.ebparks.org.

Special considerations: The road passes through open grasslands with little shade and can be brutal on hot summer days. After rainstorms the adobe soils become muddy. The park is home to rattlesnakes and mountain lions. While an encounter is unlikely, caution and common sense are advised.

Other: No water or restrooms are available along the route, so be sure to use the facilities before you set off.

Alhambra Creek Trail

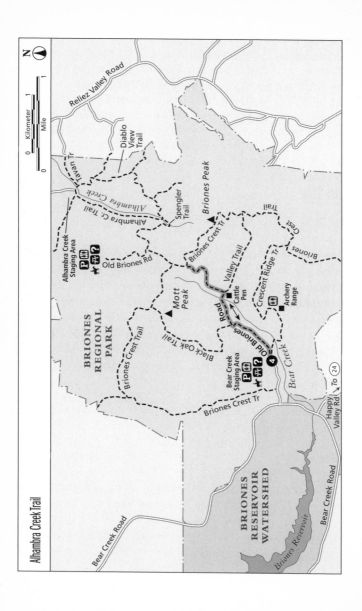

Finding the trailhead: From Highway 24 in Orinda, take the Orinda/Camino Pablo exit and head west, following Camino Pablo for 2.1 miles to its junction with Bear Creek Road. Make a right (east) turn on Bear Creek Road and go 5 miles to the signed access road for the Bear Creek Staging Area on the right (east). Follow the road for 0.4 mile to the park entry kiosk. Park in the easternmost lot, near the gated entry to the Old Briones Road. *DeLorme Northern California Atlas and Gazetteer*: Page 105 A4. GPS: N37 55.653' W122 09.323'.

The Hike

Colonial California was a land of vast ranchos. The Spanish and Mexican governments granted enormous tracts of the countryside to favored families, and those families created cattle and farming empires on what had once been the realm of tule elk, golden bears, and indigenous tribes.

By the time colonial ranching reached its height in the early 1800s, the native population had either been killed off by disease, driven into less desirable areas, or had been enslaved by missionaries and landlords. Meantime the rancho owners, like Felipe Briones, prospered.

The Briones family's ownership of the enormous rancho—the park brochure notes that more than 13,300 acres were part of a patent issued in 1878—survived the upheaval of California's transfer to the United States in the wake of the gold rush. The property was eventually acquired by public entities seeking to preserve the area as a watershed. Today the park shares a boundary with East Bay Municipal Utilities District land around Briones Reservoir, protecting a scenic and essential watershed.

And through it all cattle have grazed the meadows and hillsides . . . .

This route follows the Old Briones Road, which reaches east from the Bear Creek drainage over the Briones crest (more than 1,300 feet) into the Alhambra Valley. It climbs moderately through oaks, laurels, and buckeyes to a sprawling meadow at the base of the crest, then ascends steep hills pleated with game and livestock trails to a high point between Briones Peak (1,483 feet) on the southeast and Mott Peak (1,424 feet) on the northwest. A seat on the rustic bench in the saddle at the junction of Old Briones Road and the Briones Crest Trail affords a stunning vista west of the Bear Creek valley and the tree-shrouded east faces of the Berkeley hills. Views to the north and east spread from Mount Diablo to the Carquinez Strait, Suisun Bay, and the Sacramento River delta.

A cattle pen near the 1-mile mark testifies to the long history of grazing on the former rancho, whether cows are lowing or not. Beyond the pen the road climbs steeply, but never radically, toward the summit. Take your time with the climb and enjoy the wonderful views up and down the Bear Creek valley.

A lone bench on the summit of the crest marks the end of the route. From here, all the panoramas are spread before you. When you've taken them in, return as you came.

Miles and Directions

0.0   Start.

0.1   The paved portion of the trail (remnants of the old county road to Martinez) ends when it forks at the entrance to the Briones Archery Range (Seaborg Trail) on the right (south). Stay left (east) on the Old Briones Road, passing through a cattle gate.

0.6   Pass the sign for Fire Road 19-25 and the junction with the

Black Oak Trail on the left (north). Proceed straight (north-east) on Old Briones Road through the meadow.

0.8 Pass through a gate.

0.9 Pass a water trough and cattle pen in the shade to the right (south) of the road.

1.0 Reach the intersection with the Valley Trail. Turn sharply left (north) and begin to climb in earnest.

1.6 Arrive at the junction with the Briones Crest Trail, which traverses the ridge from northwest to northeast. A fence line and gate mark the intersection. Old Briones Road continues straight (north) into the Alhambra Valley, but turn left on a side trail alongside the fence toward a bench on the ridge crest.

1.7 The apex of this hike is the bench. Take a seat, enjoy the views, and marvel at how far (and high) you've come. Retrace your steps back down to the trailhead.

3.3 Arrive back at the trailhead and parking area.

5 Jewel Lake Loop (Tilden Regional Park)

Trade the impenetrable foliage of the riparian zone along Wildcat Creek for the crackling, littered landscape of a eucalyptus forest along the short Jewel Lake loop.

Distance: 1.1-mile loop.
Approximate hiking time: 45 minutes.
Difficulty: Easy.
Trail surface: Pavement, broad dirt road, dirt singletrack.
Best season: Year-round.
Other trail users: Trail runners.
Canine compatibility: Dogs not permitted.
Fees and permits: None.
Schedule: The park opens at 8:00 a.m. daily. A curfew is imposed between 10:00 p.m. and 5:00 a.m.
Maps: USGS Richmond; East Bay Regional Park District brochure and map available at the trailhead and at www.ebparks .org.
Trail contact: East Bay Regional Park District, 2950 Peralta Oaks Court/P.O. Box 5381, Oakland, CA 94605-0381; (888) EBPARKS; www.ebparks.org.
Special considerations: Water, restrooms, picnic facilities, a tot lot, and information are available in the Tilden Nature Area parking lot and at the Environmental Education Center, just a little way down the trail. You can also pick up a self-guided trail guide to the Jewel Lake Trail at the center (though it was not available in late 2008). If the guide is available for your visit, it describes the hike in a counterclockwise direction.
Other: Begin or end your hike with a tour of the Environmental Education Center, which features a walk-through display of the ecology and history of the Wildcat Canyon watershed including geology, flora and fauna, and human history. From conquest to coyotes, you'll find it here. The center is open Tuesday through Sunday from 10:00 a.m. to 5:00 p.m. It is also open on Monday holidays including Labor Day and Memorial Day. It is closed Christmas, Thanksgiving, and New Year's Day.

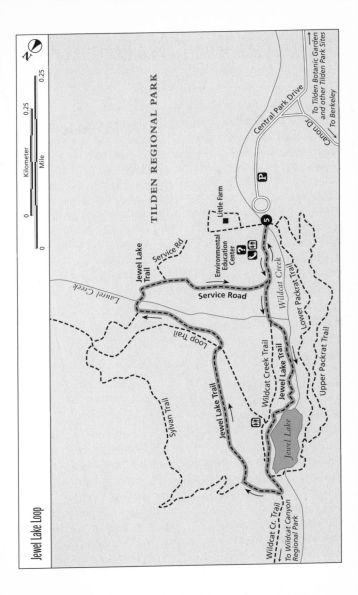

Jewel Lake Loop

TILDEN REGIONAL PARK

Little Farm

Environmental Education Center

Service Rd

Jewel Lake Trail

Laurel Creek

Service Road

Loop Trail

Sylvan Trail

Jewel Lake Trail

Wildcat Creek Trail

Jewel Lake Trail

Wildcat Creek

Lower Packrat Trail

Upper Packrat Trail

Jewel Lake

Wildcat Cr. Trail

To Wildcat Canyon
Regional Park

Central Park Drive

Canon Dr.

To Tilden Botanic Garden
and other Tilden Park Sites

To Berkeley

Kilometer

Mile

0   0.25

0   0.25

You can also visit the Little Farm, which is next door to the environmental center, and is a favorite of families with young children. Little Farm is open daily from 8:00 a.m. to 4:00 p.m.

Finding the trailhead: Tilden Regional Park's Nature Area is located just north of the intersection of Canon Drive and Central Park Drive above Berkeley. From Interstate 80 take the University Avenue exit and head east on University Avenue to Oxford Street at the University of California–Berkeley campus. Turn left (north) on Oxford Street for 1.4 miles to Marin Avenue. Turn right (east) on Marin and go 0.2 mile to Spruce Street. Turn left (north) on Spruce Street and go 0.4 mile, across Grizzly Peak Boulevard, to Canon Drive. Turn right (east) on Canon Drive and descend to Central Park Drive. Turn left (north) on Central Park Drive and into the long parking lot for the Tilden Nature Area. The trailhead is at the far north end of the lot, near the entrance to the Environmental Education Center and the Little Farm. *DeLorme Northern California Atlas & Gazetteer*: Page 104 B4. GPS: N37 54.540' W122 15.911'.

The Hike

A short meander through the dense riparian zone bordering Wildcat Creek is the highlight of this hike. A raised boardwalk tunnels through tangled growth fortified by the hidden waterway, a web of willow, alder, and berry brambles that harbors songbirds, adorable California newts, squirrels, and other creatures of the thicket.

Juxtapose this moist, lush habitat with that of the eucalyptus forest on the hillside just east of the creek—dry, smelling of spice, and dominated by a single species—and you'll get a snapshot understanding of how invasive species can alter a native environment.

The hike begins on the paved road. The Environmental Education Center and Little Farm are on the right (east); stay straight (north) toward Jewel Lake. The Jewel Lake

Trail intersection comes up quickly, dropping left onto a boardwalk that parallels hidden Wildcat Creek. For a tenth of a mile, you're enveloped in an almost prehistoric landscape thick with moss, ferns, vines, and brambles, with willow and alder arcing overhead. It ends all too soon, with a few short stairs leading up to the Wildcat Creek Trail and a narrow, shaded track that runs alongside.

Jewel Lake is a charming little pond, deep green and frequented by ducks. Hewn-log benches provide opportunities to relax and enjoy. The Jewel Lake Trail takes off to the right (east) at the north end of the lake, just beyond the dam, spillway, and junction with the Lower and Upper Packrat Trails.

The trail launches into the eucalyptus forest, climbing gently via stairs to the junction with the Sylvan Trail. Trail posts are marked with symbols rather than letters; follow the route marked with the duck. A rolling, easy traverse leads south through the peeling trees, the singletrack littered with their discarded leaves and strips of bark. Cross the unpaved Loop Trail at 0.7 mile, then drop into the Laurel Creek drainage.

Oak vie with eucalyptus as the dominant tree along the descent to Laurel Creek. The trail follows a half-buried pipeline, then drops down stairs to another junction with the Sylvan Trail. A bridge spans Laurel Creek, which runs year-round but is sluggish in late season. Climb back into eucalyptus on the other side of the creek, crossing wooden boardwalks through a little meadow and a second bridge before meeting a service road.

A quick jog across the road deposits you on the broad lawn behind the Environmental Education Center. It's a short hop from here to the trailhead and parking lot.

Miles and Directions

0.0 Start on the obvious, paved Wildcat Creek Trail. The Packrat Trail departs to the left (west)

0.1 Pass the Environmental Education Center and Little Farm on the right (east). Proceed straight (northwest) on the paved path.

0.2 Reach the Jewel Lake Trail intersection. Go left, dropping onto the boardwalk sandwiched between Wildcat Creek and the broader Wildcat Creek Trail.

0.3 Climb a few steps back to the Wildcat Creek Trail. You'll find water, restrooms, and benches at this junction. Turn left (north) toward Jewel Lake.

0.4 Pass Jewel Lake. At the dam and spillway a bridge links left (south) to the Lower and Upper Packrat Trails. Stay straight (north) on the broad dirt Wildcat Trail for about 50 yards to the Jewel Lake loop intersection on the right (east). Go right and uphill on the Jewel Lake Trail.

0.5 Two rustic flights of steps lead to the Sylvan Trail junction. Stay straight (south) on the Jewel Lake loop, marked with the duck symbol.

0.7 Cross the Loop Trail and continue on the marked Jewel Lake Trail, which drops toward Laurel Creek.

0.9 Reach the bridge over Laurel Creek and a junction with the Sylvan Trail. Cross the bridge and climb into the eucalyptus on the other side.

1.0 Meet the service road behind the Environmental Education Center. Turn right (south) on the road and continue about 50 yards to rejoin the Jewel Lake Trail, which ends on the lawn behind the environmental center.

1.1 Circle the environmental center on the paved path back to the trailhead and parking area.

6 Tilden Regional Park Botanic Garden

Tilden's botanic garden immerses visitors in the amazing diversity of California's herbal and floral heritage. It's a balm for the soul that you'll want to apply season after season.

Distance: 1 mile, more or less, of interlocking loops.
Approximate hiking time: 1 hour or all day.
Difficulty: Easy.
Trail surface: Dirt singletrack, concrete, wooden bridges and boardwalks, flagstone.
Best season: Year-round.
Other trail users: None.
Canine compatibility: Dogs not permitted.
Fees and permits: None.
Schedule: The garden is open from 8:30 a.m. to 5:00 p.m. (5:30 p.m. in summer). It is closed on Thanksgiving, Christmas, and New Year's Day.
Maps: USGS Briones Valley; East Bay Regional Park District brochure and map available at the garden visitor center and at www.ebparks.org.
Trail contact: East Bay Regional Park District, 2950 Peralta Oaks Court/P.O. Box 5381, Oakland, CA 94605-0381; (888) EBPARKS; www.ebparks.org. You can also contact Friends of the Regional Parks Botanic Garden at (510) 841-8732 or visit www.nativeplants.org; the Web site contains everything you'd ever want to know about the garden.
Special considerations: Bring along a camera to record the blooms and unusual plants you'll see along the trails. Restrooms are located in the parking area. A water fountain is at the visitor center.
Other: Garden tours are offered on most Saturdays and Sundays and begin at the visitor center at 2:00 p.m. In addition, Friends of the Regional Parks Botanic Garden sponsors a number of events and classes at the garden, including lectures and plant and seed sales. Visit www.nativeplants.org for more information.

Finding the trailhead: The botanic garden is located on Wildcat Canyon Road above Berkeley. From Interstate 80 take the Gilman Street exit and head east on Gilman Street to San Pablo Avenue. Turn left (north) on San Pablo Avenue to Marin Avenue and turn right (east). Follow Marin Avenue east for about 1.2 miles to Monterey Avenue, where you'll make a slight left to rejoin Marin Avenue. Continue on Marin for 0.6 mile to the roundabout. Go around to Marin Avenue (second right) and exit. Go another 0.7 mile up Marin Avenue to Grizzly Peak Boulevard. Turn left (north) on Grizzly Peak Boulevard for 0.1 mile to Sunset Lane. Go right (east) on Sunset Lane for 0.2 mile to Wildcat Canyon Road. Turn right (south) on Wildcat Canyon Road and go 1.1 miles to the well-signed parking area for the botanic garden on the right (west). The garden entrance is across the road from the lot.

You can also reach the park from Highway 24 in Oakland by taking the Fish Ranch Road exit and heading north on Fish Ranch Road to Grizzly Peak Boulevard. Continue north on Grizzly Peak Boulevard to South Park Drive (closed November through March). Turn right onto South Park Drive and continue to Wildcat Canyon Road and the botanic garden. *DeLorme Northern California Atlas & Gazetteer:* Page 104 B4. GPS (parking lot): N37 53.546' W122 14.572'. GPS (trailhead at visitor center): N37 53.572' W122 14.565'.

The Hike

Tilden Regional Park's botanic garden is like a theme park for nature lovers. Along its historic paths California becomes a small world, where only a few steps separate the floral wonders of the Sierra from those of the seashore.

The garden is laid out in ten sections—botanic capsules of all the plant communities within the state. Rare and endangered plants from each region, as well as more common flora, have been collected and planted on these ten acres, labeled and meticulously cared for. You'll encounter manzanita and sword fern and larkspur on your hikes in other parts of the East Bay, but here it is manicured, nurtured, and specifically identified by both its common and Latin names.

Yes, it's educational—the garden is within a stone's throw of the University of California–Berkeley, and is used for horticultural research and to conserve threatened and endangered plant species—but you'll forget that you're learning anything as you follow Wildcat Creek down into the canyon section of the garden, or climb into the cool and lofty groves of the Pacific rainforest section.

Begin your exploration in the visitor center, where you'll find displays that touch on California's natural history and the history of the botanic garden itself. Planting began in 1940, under the direction of longtime garden administrator James Roof and with the help of the Works Project Administration (a New Deal organization). Among the first sections installed on the grounds was the redwood grove, a distinctly California phenomenon, followed by plantings from the Shasta area, the Channel Islands, and southern California's deserts. Progress in the garden wasn't steady in those inaugural years, interrupted by World War II and fires and floods in the 1950s, but by the time director Roof retired in 1975, much of the infrastructure, including the landscaping and pathways, was in place.

No Miles and Directions are provided for this tour, since the trails aren't labeled, you can't get lost, and you're bound to explore as suits your whim. Circling the grounds in a vaguely counterclockwise direction, you'll encounter Joshua trees, prickly pears, and palms in the Sierra Madre Desert section, and shady ironwoods in the Channel Islands section. Drop down to Wildcat Creek via paths through either the Franciscan section, which features plants native to the San Francisco peninsula, or through the Canyon section, the garden's newest addition. Boardwalks and bridges lead through the thick foliage along the creek, and trailside benches allow you to pause and enjoy whatever blooms are tossing their scents into the air at the moment.

Climb out of the creek via easy switchbacks into the Pacific rainforest section, thick with western hemlock and ferns, fireweed, stream orchid, wild ginger, and valerian. The redwood section, harboring both coast redwoods and giant sequoias, shades the high ground above the Sierra section, where you'll find ponderosa pine and a plethora of ferns including five-fingered fern, Dudley's shield fern, and deer fern.

The Sierran section stretches across the sunny south-facing slope and includes plants that thrive on granite outcrops and in mountain meadows. The Juniper Lodge, where you may find volunteers working with seedlings—or maybe luck into purchasing some native plants for your own garden—overlooks this garden room. Trails featuring elaborate stonework and concrete work interlace the floral pockets, their intricacy sometimes drawing attention from the flowers and herbs that spill over rock walls and creep to the edges of the pathways.

Wander down from the Sierra into the Shasta-Klamath section, and then into southern California and the valley and the foothills sections. It's a short, gentle climb back to the visitor center and the trailhead from the depths of the valley, but one that may take a delightfully long time.

7 Mary Bowerman Trail (Mount Diablo State Park)

On a clear day, panoramic views from the Mary Bowerman Trail stretch west across the coastal hills to the Pacific Ocean and the curve of the earth, and east across the Central Valley to the distant peaks of the Sierra Nevada.

Distance: 0.7-mile loop.

Approximate hiking time: 1 hour including stops at interpretive sites; 0.5 hour if you walk straight through.

Difficulty: Easy.

Trail surface: Pavement, dirt singletrack.

Best season: Fall and spring. The trail can be hiked year-round, though the summit can be windy at any time and downright inhospitable during a storm.

Other trail users: Trail runners.

Canine compatibility: Dogs not permitted.

Fees and permits: Entrance fees are $7 per vehicle; $6 for seniors.

Schedule: 8:00 a.m. to sunset. Watch the time so you don't get locked in at night.

Maps: USGS Clayton; Mount Diablo State Park trail map.

Trail contact: Mount Diablo State Park, 96 Mitchell Canyon Road, Clayton, CA 94517; (925) 837-2525; www.parks.ca.gov. The Mount Diablo Interpretive Association can be contacted by writing P.O. Box 346, Walnut Creek, CA 94597-0346.

Special considerations: This is rattlesnake country, but the snakes won't bite if you don't bother them. After all, you're way too big for dinner. Watch the weather; it can be changeable on the summit and very different from that in the valley. Dress in layers and bring extra clothing if hiking in winter. If snow is going to fall in the Bay Area, it'll lay thickest on the summit of Diablo.

Other: Stop in at the picturesque summit visitor center, which houses interpretive displays describing the mountain's human

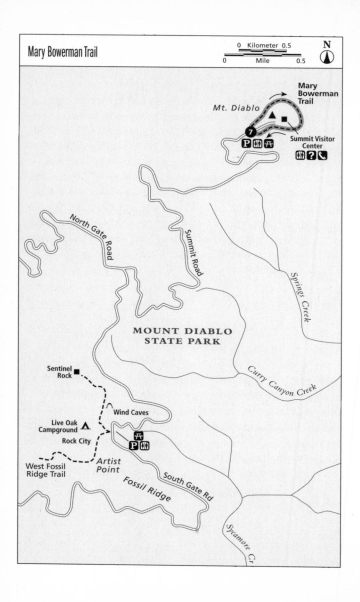

Mary Bowerman Trail

0 Kilometer 0.5
0 Mile 0.5

N

Mt. Diablo

Mary Bowerman Trail

7

P

Summit Visitor Center

North Gate Road

Summit Road

Springs Creek

MOUNT DIABLO STATE PARK

Sentinel Rock

Curry Canyon Creek

Wind Caves

Live Oak Campground

Rock City

P

West Fossil Ridge Trail

Artist Point

Fossil Ridge

South Gate Rd

Sycamore Cr

history and ecology. The must-visit observation deck caps the center. Hours are from 10:00 a.m. to 4:00 p.m. every day.

Finding the trailhead: From Interstate 680 in Danville, take the Diablo Road/Danville exit. Go east on Diablo Road. At the intersection with El Cerro Boulevard, at 0.8 mile, turn right on Diablo Road, and follow it another 2.2 miles. At the 3-mile mark go left (east) on the steep, winding Mount Diablo Scenic Boulevard, which becomes South Gate Road once you enter the park at 4 miles. The entrance station is at 5.7 miles. At 8.8 miles, arrive at the intersection with North Gate Road, which leads down into Walnut Creek. Go right (up and generally northeast) on South Gate Road for another 4.6 miles to the upper summit area parking lot (13.4 miles total). *DeLorme Northern California Atlas & Gazetteer:* Page 105 A6. GPS: N37 52.884' W121 54.874'.

The Hike

The summit of Mount Diablo is more than 3,800 feet above sea level, and more than a thousand feet higher than its nearest neighbor. So it should come as no surprise that the views from the top—especially on a clear day—are superlative.

The Mary Bowerman Trail circumnavigates the summit, offering the same views you'll find at the observation deck on the peak's apex with the added benefit of a natural history lesson and a chance to stretch your legs after the long, adventurous drive to the trailhead.

Begin the hike in the lower summit parking lot, which is about 0.1 mile downhill from the smaller visitor center parking area. The trailhead for the self-guided Mary Bowerman Trail, also known as the Fire Interpretive Trail, is about 30 yards above and left (northeast) of the parking lot entrance, across the road and adjacent to a small picnic area.

You can see the trail's end from the parking entrance as well, to the right (southeast).

Pick up a guide at the trailhead and head off into the oak scrubland that encompasses the first section of the route. Pass the first interpretive marker almost immediately; this describes the habitat you are traveling through. The markers are wooden posts with white tops, and can't be missed.

Beyond marker 2 (beware the poison oak), views open of the quarry on Mount Zion, Suisun Bay, and into the Central Valley and beyond. Marker 3 will draw your attention—at least momentarily—away from the views and to the stone bed that underlies the paved path. At the 0.1-mile mark you'll reach a pullout with more views, then markers 4 and 5, for greywacke (as opposed to greyserious) and chert (which is not something that birds do).

Beyond a viewing area with a scope the trail turns to dirt and swings onto the east face of the summit. The summit observation deck is above and to the right. Oak scrub provides pockets of welcome shade on a hot summer day. Signs of a 1977 fire that charred this face are long gone, covered by brushy, fragrant chaparral.

At the trail's halfway point, where the path arcs onto the mountain's south face and offers views of the Oakland hills, the Golden Gate, and the distant Pacific, you'll pass the impressive Devil's Pulpit. Resist the temptation to climb the pulpit, as the rock is crumbly and unstable.

You'll pass markers 10 (which marks the advent of the grassland plant community) and 11 as you traverse the west face. The trail is exposed in places and might give pause to hikers with vertigo. A gentle ascent begins at marker 12 and continues all the way to trail's end at 0.7 mile. Drop quickly from the trail into the parking lot.

Miles and Directions

0.0 Start.

0.1 Pass the first few interpretive markers to a viewpoint on the paved path. Proceed past markers 4 and 5.

0.25 Reach a viewing station at marker 6; you can use the scope to zoom in on distant landmarks including Sierra Nevada peaks. The trail turns to dirt and views open onto the Sacramento and San Joaquin River deltas, blue veins on a skin of gold or green, depending on the season.

0.4 Round onto the south face at marker 9, passing the Devil's Pulpit. Other, lower rock outcrops make great viewing platforms. Social trails head to various outcrops, but the route proper is well marked with an arrow and trail sign.

0.5 Traverse across the south face. The trail begins an easy ascent past the last five interpretive markers, which describe the changing habitat and some of the flora that thrives on the slope.

0.7 Arrive at the end of the trail. Drop down the paved road into the parking area.

8 Rock City and West Fossil Ridge Trail (Mount Diablo State Park)

Explore Rock City's Wind Caves, sandstone rock outcrops that have been sculpted by wind, water, and time, then head off on an easy, secluded walk through the woods to a viewpoint at the end of West Fossil Ridge.

Distance: 1.6 miles out and back for the West Fossil Ridge Trail; Rock City is about 0.6 mile out and back.

Approximate hiking time: 1.5 hours.

Difficulty: Moderate due to tricky sandstone walking surfaces and short steep pitches.

Trail surface: Dirt road, dirt singletrack, sandstone.

Best season: Spring, summer, and fall. Winter rain may make the trails slick and muddy.

Other trail users: Trail runners, climbers, mountain bikers.

Canine compatibility: Dogs not permitted.

Fees and permits: Entrance fees are $7 per vehicle; $6 for seniors.

Schedule: 8:00 a.m. to sunset. Keep a close watch on the time so you don't get locked in at night.

Maps: USGS Clayton; Mount Diablo State Park trail map.

Trail contact: Mount Diablo State Park, 96 Mitchell Canyon Road, Clayton, CA 94517; (925) 837-2525; www.parks.ca.gov. The Mount Diablo Interpretive Association can be reached by writing P.O. Box 346, Walnut Creek, CA 94597-0346.

Special considerations: This is rattlesnake country, but the snakes will only bite if you harass them. After all, you're way too big for dinner.

Other: You'll find water and a map of the area in the trailhead parking lot. Overnight camping facilities are available in the Rock City area; contact the park for more information.

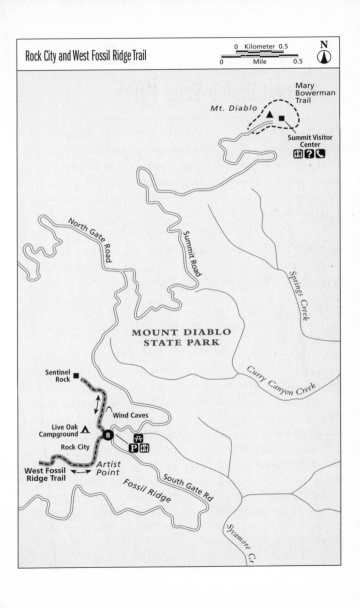

Rock City and West Fossil Ridge Trail

0   Kilometer   0.5
0   Mile   0.5

N

Mary Bowerman Trail

Mt. Diablo

Summit Visitor Center

North Gate Road

Summit Road

Springs Creek

MOUNT DIABLO STATE PARK

Curry Canyon Creek

Sentinel Rock

Wind Caves

Live Oak Campground

8

Rock City

West Fossil Ridge Trail

Artist Point

South Gate Rd

Fossil Ridge

Sycamore Cr

Finding the trailhead: From Interstate 680 in Danville, take the Diablo Road/Danville exit. Go east on Diablo Road. At the intersection with El Cerro Boulevard, at 0.8 mile, turn right, remaining on Diablo Road, and follow it another 2.2 miles. At the 3-mile mark, go left (east) on steep, winding Mount Diablo Scenic Boulevard, which becomes South Gate Road once you enter the park at a gate at 4 miles. Reach the entrance station at 5.7 miles. The Rock City parking lots and picnic areas, along with the Live Oak Campground and trailheads, are 1 mile from the entrance kiosk at 6.7 miles. There are several parking lots at Rock City; park in the lot serving the Big Rock Picnic Area, at the top of the access road to Live Oak Campground. Trail descriptions begin from this lot. *DeLorme Northern California Atlas & Gazetteer:* Page 105 A6. GPS: N37 50.934' W121 56.000'.

The Hike

These two trails explore vastly different landscapes within a small section of the park. You can take the trails in either order, or simply do one or the other. Rock City will delight children, so if one hike is all your family can manage, stick with it. Hardier children of all ages will enjoy linking the two. The Rock City exploration is presented first, followed by a description of the West Fossil Ridge Trail.

To reach the Wind Caves and Sentinel Rock, head up and right (north) on the dirt track alongside the paved roadway. Lots of social trails intermingle in this area; if you head left (west) toward the first obvious rock formations, you can scramble down to the Elephant Rock Picnic Area and its huge cave-like alcove with sandstone "tusks" overhanging the entrance.

The Wind Caves are above the Big Rock Picnic Area, where you'll find an interpretive billboard and a marker for the Trail Through Time. Walk left (west) on the Trail Through Time alongside a 100-foot sandstone wall where wind and water have carved nearly perfectly circular alcoves, some standing alone, some linked by threads of rock. These hollows freckle the sandstone, making perfect perches for children.

Rock City's Trail Through Time hitches right (east) around the end of the Wind Caves wall. Social trails lead to a cluster of rocks that offer great views and tempting scrambling, but don't venture onto the heights unless you are an experienced climber.

The narrow dirt track continues through oak woodlands to a trail fork; stay left (north) and head uphill to the trail's end at Sentinel Rock and the junction with the CCC Trail. Pull up a flat section of rock and enjoy views north across the slopes of Mount Diablo, which are pocked with similar outcrops. Return as you came, arriving back at the lower parking lot at 0.6 mile.

The West Fossil Ridge Trail begins 0.1 mile down the paved access road to the Live Oak Campground. The broad track, labeled Fire Road 59-2 as well as West Fossil Ridge, takes off to the left (northwest). Easy to follow, it leads up through oak woodlands to a meadow, past the Artist Point Trail, then climbs into the shade and traverses a forested hillside that is aflame with red-leaved poison oak toward the end of summer. Thankfully, the road is so wide you'll never get close to it. Breaks in the canopy offer glimpses of Rock City to the south and east, and Sonoma Mountain and Mount St. Helena to the north and west.

A switchback at the end of the ridge swings you onto the west face. Head south and downhill through the grasslands to a saddle, then up a steep slope littered with brittle cones dropped by a pair of lonesome pines. The trail flattens on the final stretch, ending on a scrubby ridgetop at an "end of trail" marker (0.8 mile). The steep slopes that make up the view are covered in chaparral plants like chamise that burn brown by the end of summer, a dark felt coat laid across the mountain's shoulders. Return as you came.

Miles and Directions

Rock City, Wind Caves, and Sentinel Rock

0.0 Start.

0.1 Reach the Wind Caves. At the end of the wall, a trail marker points right (east), and the dirt singletrack leads past several more Trail Through Time markers toward Sentinel Rock.

0.2 The trail climbs on sandstone to a flat area with another rock outcrop on the left (west). Stay left (north) past the Trail Through Time marker.

0.3 Arrive at Sentinel Rock and the junction with the CCC Trail. Enjoy the views, then return as you came.

0.6 Reach the parking area.

West Fossil Ridge Trail

0.0 Start by dropping downhill from the parking area on the paved access road to Live Oak Campground.

0.1 Reach the start of the trail proper, at the intersection with Fire Road 59-2. Go left (northwest) and uphill on the fire road.

0.3 A gentle ascent leads to a lovely meadow and the junction with the Artist Point Trail, which departs to the left (southeast). Stay straight (north) on the fire road.

0.4 Pass a singletrack social trail on the left (northwest); again, stay on the fire road.

0.6 Round the end of the ridge and begin a descent through grasslands to a saddle. The road climbs steeply from the saddle past two pines.

0.8 An "end of trail" marker denotes the turnaround point on top of the ridge. Return as you came.

1.6 Arrive back at the trailhead above the Live Oak Campground.

9 Volvon/Blue Oak Trail Loop (Morgan Territory Regional Preserve)

The distance between the developed areas of the East Bay and the Morgan Territory can be measured in more than miles. It can also be captured in peace and quiet, which is commonplace on these secluded trails.

Distance: 3.6-mile loop.
Approximate hiking time: 2 hours.
Difficulty: Moderate due to distance.
Trail surface: Dirt and gravel ranch roads.
Best season: Spring and fall.
Other trail users: Cyclists, equestrians, trail runners, cows.
Canine compatibility: Leashed dogs permitted in developed areas. Dogs may run off-leash on trails.
Fees and permits: None.
Schedule: The park opens at 8:00 a.m. daily. Specific closing hours are posted at the park entrance. A curfew is imposed between 10:00 p.m. and 5:00 a.m.
Maps: USGS Tassajara; East Bay Regional Park District brochure and map available at the trailhead and at www.ebparks.org.
Trail contact: East Bay Regional Park District, 2950 Peralta Oaks Court/P.O. Box 5381, Oakland, CA 94605-0381; (888) EBPARKS; www.ebparks.org.
Special considerations: The park is home to rattlesnakes and mountain lions. While an encounter is unlikely, caution and common sense are advised.
Other: There are no amenities along the route. Use restrooms and fill water bottles at the trailhead.

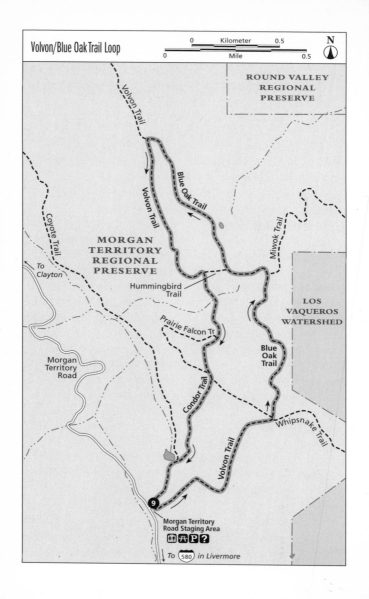

Volvon/Blue Oak Trail Loop

Kilometer
Mile

N

ROUND VALLEY
REGIONAL
PRESERVE

Volvon Trail

Blue Oak Trail

Volvon Trail

Miwok Trail

Coyote Trail

MORGAN
TERRITORY
REGIONAL
PRESERVE

To
Clayton

Hummingbird
Trail

LOS
VAQUEROS
WATERSHED

Prairie Falcon Tr

Morgan
Territory
Road

Condor Trail

Blue
Oak
Trail

Whipsnake Trail

Volvon Trail

9

Morgan Territory
Road Staging Area

To 580 in Livermore

Finding the trailhead: To reach the trailhead from Interstate 680 in Walnut Creek, take the Ygnacio Valley Road exit. Head east on Ygnacio Valley Road for 7 miles to Clayton Road. Turn right (southeast) on Clayton Road for 2.5 miles to where it becomes Marsh Creek Road. Continue on Marsh Creek Road for 3.4 miles to Morgan Territory Road. Turn right (south) on Morgan Territory Road and travel 9.2 miles to the park entrance, parking lot, and trailhead on the left (north). The address is 9401 Morgan Territory Road in Livermore. *DeLorme Northern California Atlas and Gazetteer*: Page 105 B7. GPS: N37 49.115' W121 47.738'.

The Hike

Draped across the hilly backside of the Diablo range, the hills and hollows of Morgan Territory Regional Preserve are a rare prize, a quiet tucked-away treasure of expansive vistas and wildflower fields.

The park harbors a perfect confluence of seclusion and great scenery, but arguably its most significant feature is the solitude. Morgan Territory lies outside the busy interstate corridors that define the East Bay, rendering trail traffic light and expanding options for hikers seeking a quiet, contemplative trek.

The territory was once the homestead of Jeremiah Morgan, a forty-niner who, after trying his hand at gold mining, opted to take on the equally rigorous occupation of rancher. The trails you travel on this route are former ranch roads. Before that—and before the arrival of the Spanish in the late 1700s—the land was cultivated and harvested by the native Volvon tribe.

While late fall is a great time to visit, as the sycamores and big-leaf maples along Marsh Creek turn sunset colors, spring is high time for wildflower displays. The park boasts that more than ninety species of wildflowers bloom in its meadows, among them the rare Diablo sunflower. Another rarity, the endangered Alameda whipsnake, also can be found in the park . . . not to mention tarantulas that traverse the trails in autumn looking for mates. It's a rich and diverse habitat.

This loop can be hiked in either direction, but is described here counterclockwise beginning on the Volvon Trail. This ranch road rolls through open meadows dotted with oaks and rock outcrops that poke gray, lichen-stained heads out of the grass.

Abandon the Volvon Trail for the Blue Oak Trail at the 0.8-mile mark, swinging through a swale cropped close by cattle. Crest the shoulder of a hill and views open down onto the Sacramento River delta. Travel down and around through more grasslands to views of Mount Diablo; head up and over to more bay and delta views at a stunning oak. This section of the route is a festival of vistas.

Beyond the junction with the Hummingbird Trail the oaks gradually become more tightly packed on the land-scape. Swing past a pond as you near the junction with the Volvon/Bob Walker/Diablo Regional Trails. You'll follow the Volvon Trail (still a ranch road) south and back toward the trailhead. Views now include the east-facing flanks of Mount Diablo; the summit may be shrouded in clouds on stormy days.

The Volvon Trail meets the Condor Trail in a small meadow; turn right (southwest) on the Condor singletrack to enjoy some challenging walking through the drainage of the seasonal stream, and over-the-shoulder views of Mount Diablo. The Condor Trail leads past a small reed-filled pond, then up to the trailhead and parking area.

Miles and Directions

0.0 Start. The first trail junction is about 100 yards from the parking area; go right (northeast) through the gate on the signed Volvon Trail (also the Bob Walker Regional Trail).

0.2 Arrive at the junction with a dirt road and go right (northeast). Crest a small hill and drop through a gully shaded by beautiful dome-crowned oaks.

0.4 Merge onto the gravel road (signed Volvon Trail), heading left (north). Social and cattle trails intersect the route; stay straight on the obvious road/trail.

0.8 Reach the Whipsnake Trail junction and go left (north) on the Volvon Trail. The intersection with the Blue Oak Trail is about 100 yards beyond. Go right (north) on the Blue Oak Trail. Pass a social trail as you arc through a swale; radio towers rise on the high point to the right (east). Once out of the swale, views open and accompany you for a half mile.

1.3 Arrive at the junction with the Miwok Trail (Diablo Regional Trail). Go left (northwest) on the Blue Oak Trail. Remain on the obvious broad road past side trails that offer potential cut-offs; you won't want to miss a foot of the trek.

1.5 At the Hummingbird Trail junction, stay right (northwest) on the Blue Oak Trail (now part of the Diablo Regional Trail). The Hummingbird Trail offers a loop-shortening option, crossing westward to link with the Volvon Trail and taking more than a mile off the hike distance.

1.7 Pass a pond on the right (east). The gentle downhill run turns into a brief climb, then flattens and descends through more oaks and lichen-covered rock outcrops.

2.1 Arrive at the junction with the Volvon Trail (also the Bob Walker and Diablo Regional Trails). Turn left (south) and uphill on the broad Volvon Trail.

2.6 Pass the junction with the Hummingbird Trail; social trails also intersect the Volvon Trail in this area. Stay straight (south) on the Volvon Trail.

2.8 Reach the junction with the Prairie Falcon singletrack. Stay left (southeast) on the Volvon Trail. Prairie Falcon reaches out to a brushy overlook, then returns to the main Volvon track.

3.0 Pass the second junction with the Prairie Falcon Trail and arrive at the Condor Trail junction. At this intersection you'll find a restroom, picnic table, and the rusted remnants of farming apparatus. Turn right (southwest) on the Condor Trail, passing through a seasonal drainage shaded by manzanita and traversing an open hillside that offers views back to Mount Diablo.

3.4 Drop through a ravine and cross a wooden bridge over a seasonal stream, then arrive at the junction of the Condor Trail and the Coyote Trail. Turn right (south) on the Coyote Trail, passing through a gate. An overgrown pond is on the right (west).

3.5 The Coyote Trail meets the Volvon Trail after climbing along a fence line with the trailhead parking area in sight. Turn right (south) on the Volvon Trail.

3.6 Arrive back at the parking lot.

10 Round Top Loop Trail (Sibley Volcanic Regional Preserve)

An easy circumnavigation of Round Top peak features lovely views of San Francisco Bay and Mount Diablo and interesting insights into the geology of a long-extinct volcano.

Distance: 1.6-mile lollipop.

Approximate hiking time: 1 hour.

Difficulty: Easy.

Trail surface: Paved and gravel roads.

Best season: Spring, summer, and fall. Winter rains may create muddy conditions on unpaved trail sections.

Other trail users: Runners, mountain bikers.

Canine compatibility: Leashed dogs permitted in the parking lot and at the visitor center. Dogs may be unleashed elsewhere (but owners must carry a leash).

Fees and permits: None.

Schedule: The park is open from 5:00 a.m. to 10:00 p.m. unless otherwise posted. The parking lot may be closed at 6:00 p.m. from November through March.

Maps: USGS Oakland East; East Bay Regional Park District map and brochure available online and at the trailhead.

Trail contact: East Bay Regional Park District (EBRPD), 2950 Peralta Oaks Court/P.O. Box 5381, Oakland, CA 94605-0381; (888) EBPARKS; www.ebparks.org.

Other: Be sure to check out the interpretive displays at the trailhead, which describe the park's flora and fauna and include a geologic timeline of the Berkeley hills. The EBRPD also publishes a guide to the Volcanic Trail, which can be downloaded from the Web site or purchased by contacting the district. Steve Edwards's "A Self-Guided Tour of Round Top Volcanics" is published within the park brochure.

Round Top Loop Trail

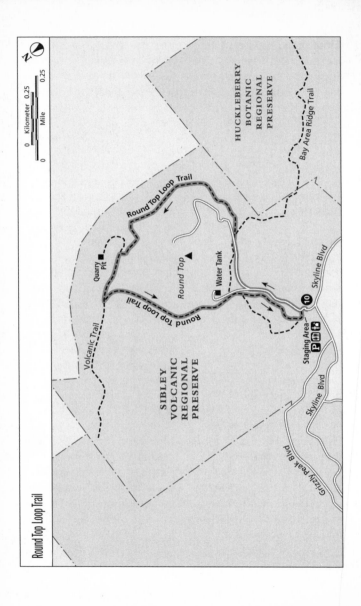

0   Kilometer   0.25

0   Mile   0.25

Round Top Loop Trail

Quarry Pit

Volcanic Trail

Round Top

Water Tank

Round Top Loop Trail

SIBLEY VOLCANIC REGIONAL PRESERVE

HUCKLEBERRY BOTANIC REGIONAL PRESERVE

Bay Area Ridge Trail

Skyline Blvd

10

Staging Area

Skyline Blvd

Grizzly Peak Blvd

Finding the trailhead: The park is located at 6800 Skyline Boulevard in the Oakland hills. From Highway 24 in Oakland, take the Highway 13 exit. Follow Highway 13 south for 0.4 mile to the Broadway Terrace exit. Go left on Broadway Terrace, and follow it east for about 2 miles up into the hills, passing a number of intersections with residential streets as you climb. When you reach Skyline Boulevard turn right (south), and follow Skyline about 1 mile to the park entrance on the left. Alternatively, follow Highway 24 through the Caldecott Tunnel to the Fish Ranch Road exit. Follow Fish Ranch Road to Grizzly Peak Boulevard, and turn left (south) on Grizzly Peak. Follow Grizzly Peak Boulevard, then Skyline Boulevard south for 2.4 miles to the park entrance on the left (east). *DeLorme Northern California Atlas & Gazetteer.* Page 105 A4. GPS: N37 50.836' W122 11.980'.

The Hike

The gentlest volcano you'll ever hike, Round Top distinguishes itself from neighboring heights in the Oakland and Berkeley hills by virtue of its fascinating geological history.

The volcano was a cauldron of activity about ten million years ago, when it spewed the various lavas (tuffs, basalts, breccias) that underlie the current landscape. Pressure from nearby earthquake faults have lifted and twisted the old volcano over the eons, exposing its innards for the education and enjoyment of scholars and hikers alike.

The Round Top Loop Trail skirts the summit of the peak. It begins on the paved road to the summit, climbing through a mixed forest of oak, manzanita, and bay laurel as it traverses the volcano's south-facing slope, and offering views into the forested canyons of neighboring Huckleberry Botanic Regional Preserve. Just before the 0.4-mile mark, the unsigned Round Top Loop Trail breaks off to the right (southeast), leaving behind the paved route. The singletrack traverses through pines, oaks, and eucalyptus;

the understory is thick with poison oak, so be sure to stay on the path.

Rounding the east face of the volcano, climb a short steep pitch through a meadow (look for wildflowers in spring) and pass through a gate, closing it behind you. Ascending through the grasslands, you'll enjoy lovely views east to Mount Diablo. The quarries that delved into Round Top are visible ahead. Top out at nearly 1,600 feet, where a short side path leads to an overlook, then descend to a trail intersection at 1 mile.

Before you head left (north) on the broad dirt roadway, check out the views from interpretive site #4. A fence at the edge of the cliff looks out over the quarry pit, which can be reached via a short, steep descent. At the bottom lie several labyrinths—stone meditation rings—the largest decorating the floor of the pit. The interpretive guide notes that the excavations here exposed the interior of the old volcano, giving researchers an inside look at its makeup.

Follow the dirt road north to the next trail crossing at 1.1 miles. Turn sharply left (southwest) on the broad Round Top Loop Trail; the Volcanic Trail goes straight (north). Continue past interpretive marker #2, which marks a portion of the volcano's caldera. Traverse through grassland and chaparral to the west face and another cattle gate. At a four-way trail intersection, bear right (southwest) on either the pavement or one of two dirt tracks; all lead down to the trailhead at 1.6 miles.

Miles and Directions

0.0 Start.

0.1 Stay right at the first trail intersection.

0.3 Pass the Ridge Trail, remaining on the paved road.

0.4 Go right (southeast) on the unmarked dirt Round Top Loop Trail. When you pass the gate in the hillside meadow, be sure to close it behind you.

1.0 Arrive at the trail intersection above the quarry pit. Go left (north) on the Round Top Loop Trail.

1.1 At the intersection with the Volcanic Trail, go sharply left (southwest) on the Round Top Loop Trail. When you reach the gate, be sure to close it behind you.

1.5 Reach the four-way trail intersection and head right (west) toward the trailhead.

1.6 Arrive at the trailhead and parking lot.

11 Rocky Ridge Loop (Las Trampas Regional Wilderness)

A challenging climb leads to a ridgetop ramble that offers expansive views west over San Francisco Bay and east to Mount Diablo and beyond.

Distance: 3.7-mile lollipop.
Approximate hiking time: 2 hours.
Difficulty: More challenging due to the steep climb to the ridgetop and the equally steep descent.
Trail surface: Paved and dirt roadway, dirt singletrack.
Best season: Spring and fall.
Other trail users: Trail runners, equestrians on the paved portion of Rocky Ridge View Trail; equestrians and cows on the unpaved Rocky Ridge View and Cuesta Trails.
Canine compatibility: Leashed dogs permitted. Dogs may run off-leash in undeveloped areas and on trails.
Fees and permits: None.
Schedule: The park is open from 5:00 a.m. to 10:00 p.m. daily unless different hours are posted at the gate.

Maps: USGS Las Trampas Ridge; East Bay Regional Park District brochure and map available at the trailhead and at www.ebparks.org.
Trail contact: East Bay Regional Park District, 2950 Peralta Oaks Court/P.O. Box 5381, Oakland, CA 94605-0381; (888) EBPARKS; www.ebparks.org.
Special considerations: The park is home to rattlesnakes and mountain lions. While an encounter is unlikely, caution and common sense are advised. You are likely, however, to encounter cows along the trail. No worries—they are gentle creatures grazing the annual grasses to reduce fire danger.
Other: There is no water along the route, so bring what you need. Use restrooms at the trailhead. The trail and ridgetop may be baking hot in summer; winter winds and rain may render them

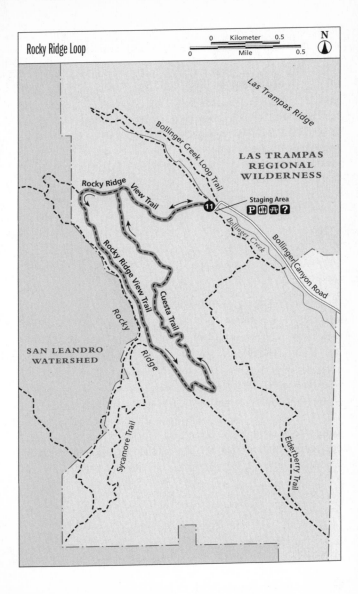

Rocky Ridge Loop

0   Kilometer   0.5

0   Mile   0.5

N

Las Trampas Ridge

Bollinger Creek Loop Trail

LAS TRAMPAS
REGIONAL
WILDERNESS

Rocky Ridge View Trail

Staging Area

11

Bollinger Creek

Bollinger Canyon Road

Rocky Ridge View Trail

Cuesta Trail

Rocky Ridge

SAN LEANDRO
WATERSHED

Sycamore Trail

Elderberry Trail

inhospitable in winter. Rain may also make the adobe trail sur- face of Cuesta Trail stickier than bubblegum on a hot sidewalk.

Finding the trailhead: The park is at 18012 Bollinger Canyon Road in San Ramon. From Interstate 680, take the Crow Canyon Road exit. Head west on Crow Canyon Road for 1.1 miles to Bollinger Canyon Road. Go right (northwest) on Bollinger Canyon Road for 3.9 miles to the Las Trampas Regional Wilderness boundary. The road leads another 0.4 mile to the Bollinger Canyon Staging Area at the road's end. The trailhead is at the gate across the paved trail at the north end of the lot. *DeLorme Northern California Atlas & Gazetteer:* Page 105 B5 and C5. GPS: N37 48.970' W122 03.017'.

The Hike

This one climbs straight up and straight down, but what lies between is superlative. The top of Rocky Ridge, like so many of the high points in the East Bay, encompasses panoramic vistas across San Francisco Bay, south along the peninsula to the rolling hills of the South Bay, around east to Mount Diablo and the Sacramento River delta, and north to Mount Tamalpais and its environs.

Not for the weak of knee, lung, or resolve, those willing and able to take on the challenge of the climb and descent will find the strenuousness mitigated by the wildflower displays on the ridge's grassy slopes. Hikers can also contemplate the area's interesting geology: Two features that define the park, Las Trampas Ridge with its dark wrap of chaparral plants and Bollinger Creek, share names with earthquake faults that shaped the landscape. The steepness of the terrain can be attributed in part to uplift along the fault lines.

The hike begins by climbing the paved Rocky Ridge View Trail. Though steep, somehow it feels easier by dint of the pavement. Go figure . . . . Once you reach the Cuesta Trail you have a choice; you can continue up the Rocky Ridge View Trail or take the loop in the other (clockwise) direction. The route is described counterclockwise, beginning with the Rocky Ridge View Trail and ending with the Cuesta Trail.

The Rocky Ridge View Trail arcs south and narrows to singletrack as it climbs the last pitch to the ridgetop. This is wildflower country, with the first blooms of lupine and poppy following close on the first moisture of the rainy season in late fall. Alternating displays continue through summer. It also affords a preview of the views above, with Mount Diablo and the San Ramon Valley in its sights.

On the ridgetop you are treated to the same views that the raptors enjoy—with the added benefit of being able to identify hawks from their topsides rather than from underneath. Turn a circle and take it all in, then continue down the trail and do it again. You won't tire of the vistas.

The trail flattens on the ridge and rollercoasters southwest through rangeland to the Cuesta Trail junction. The singletrack rounds a steep switchback, then dives toward the canyon floor, tripping in and out of folds in the hillside that are shaded with oaks, bay laurels, big leaf maples, and buckeyes. The trail can be dusty in the dry season and muddy in the wet.

The Cuesta Trail ends back on the paved Rocky Ridge View Trail; a right (southeast) turn and a quick descent land you back at the trailhead and parking area.

Miles and Directions

0.0 Start.

0.2 Cross a cattle guard and pass a social trail, continuing up on paved Rocky Ridge View Trail.

0.6 Reach the junction with the Cuesta Trail just beyond a bend in the trail, where views open north down Bollinger Canyon. Cuesta Trail is the return route; stay right (up and northeast) on either the paved road or the signed dirt singletrack that parallels the roadway.

0.8 Arrive at the junction of the Rocky Ridge View Trail and the gated trail into the adjoining San Leandro Watershed. To hike in the watershed, you must get a permit from the East Bay Municipal Utilities District (EBMUD). Go left (south) on the narrow Rocky Ridge View Trail.

1.0 Arrive at the summit of the ridge, at 1,899 feet. Pass a gated trail that leads onto EBMUD land as you head southwest on the Rocky Ridge View Trail.

1.5 Pass a Rocky Ridge View Trail marker and continue southeast on the ridge, now a dirt roadway.

1.6 Pass the Sycamore Trail in a saddle. Stay straight (southeast) on the ridgetop road.

1.8 Arrive at the junction with the Cuesta Trail. Go left (northeast) on the Cuesta Trail, which drops steeply across the east face of the ridge.

2.2 After a brief climb pass the remnant of a barbed-wire fence.

2.6 At an unmarked junction with a social trail, stay right (down and east) on the Cuesta Trail.

2.9 A copse of big old oaks and bay laurels shelters a seasonal stream and water hole.

3.3 A last stretch of singletrack through grasslands prickly with invasive star thistle in fall leads to the junction with the paved roadway. This is the end of the loop; turn right on the Rocky Ridge View Trail and descend toward the trailhead.

3.7 Arrive back at the trailhead and parking area.

12 Stream Trail (Redwood Regional Park)

Grand stands of coast redwoods, their canopies throwing down shade as thick as a flannel blanket, thrive on the banks of Redwood Creek. The Stream Trail meanders through their midst and, on a foggy day, through the mist that sustains them.

Distance: 3.0 miles out and back.

Approximate hiking time: 1.5 hours.

Difficulty: Easy.

Trail surface: Pavement, wide dirt track.

Best season: Year-round.

Other trail users: Trail runners, equestrians, cyclists to the Trail's End picnic area.

Canine compatibility: Leashed dogs permitted.

Fees and permits: Fees are charged when the park's entry kiosk is staffed. The cost is $5 per car. A $2 dog fee is levied.

Schedule: The park is open from 5:00 a.m. to 10:00 p.m. daily, unless different hours are posted at the park entry. A curfew is imposed between 10:00 p.m. and 5:00 a.m.

Maps: USGS Oakland East; East Bay Regional Park District brochure and map available at the trailhead and at www.ebparks .org.

Trail contact: East Bay Regional Park District, 2950 Peralta Oaks Court/P.O. Box 5381, Oakland, CA 94605-0381; (888) EBPARKS; www.ebparks.org.

Special considerations: Dogs must remain on leashes in this park, to protect the fragile restored stream habitat of native rainbow trout.

Other: A number of picnic areas line the route, many of them outfitted with restrooms, trash cans, interpretive signs, and water.

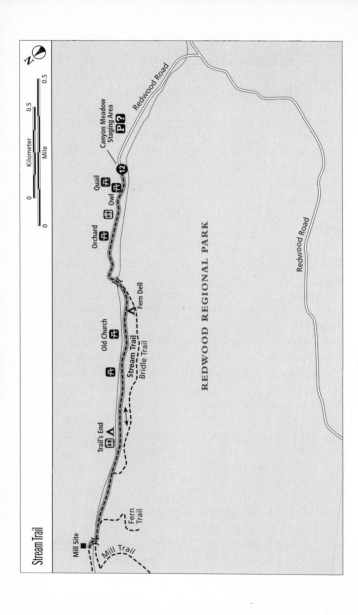

Stream Trail

Mill Site

Mill Trail

Fern Trail

Trail's End

Old Church

Stream Trail
Bridle Trail

Fern Dell

Orchard

Owl

Quail

12

Canyon Meadow
Staging Area

P ?

Redwood Road

Redwood Road

REDWOOD REGIONAL PARK

N

Kilometer
0   0.5

Mile
0   0.5

Finding the trailhead: From Interstate 580 in Oakland, take Highway 24 east toward Walnut Creek. Follow Highway 24 to the exit for Highway 13 southbound. Follow Highway 13 south to the Joaquin Miller Road/Lincoln Avenue exit. Turn left (east) on Joaquin Miller Road. Follow Joaquin Miller Road, which becomes Skyline Boulevard, for 1.8 miles to Redwood Road. Turn left (east) on Redwood Road and wind east for 2.5 miles to a left-hand (north) turn into Redwood Regional Park. Follow the park road for 0.5 mile to the Canyon Meadow Staging Area at road's end. The trailhead is at the north boundary of the parking lot. *DeLorme Northern California Atlas & Gazetteer*: Page 105 B4. GPS: N37 48.415' W122 08.931'.

The Hike

There's not a human being on the planet that wouldn't be awed standing in a forest of California redwoods. The great trees are quieting; they seem old even when they're not, wise no matter what their age. They remind you of how little you are, and how beautiful the world can be.

The redwoods along the Stream Trail in Redwood Regional Park are second- and third- generation clones of their forebears. Those ancestral trees were harvested back in the mid–1800s during the gold rush years, when nearby San Francisco was a boom town. According to park literature, the first-generation redwoods were so huge they were used by ship captains to navigate in San Francisco Bay. Five mills in the future Redwood Regional Park brought the massive sequoias down; the mills are gone now, but the clones of the ancestors live on. The trees you'll pass on this route reach as tall as 100 feet, and though they can't be distinguished from the Golden Gate, you'll still be impressed.

The trail is easy and straightforward, tracing the course of Redwood Creek. The stream, dry in late summer, is the spawning ground for descendants of a native population of rainbow trout. The trout used to follow the waterway all the way to the bay, but with the construction of dams that created Lake Chabot in 1870 and San Leandro Reservoir in the 1960s, the fish now migrate to the lakes and back. The area is designated a resource protection area for the sake of the trout.

The trail begins by passing through a series of picnic grounds, with the stream on the west side hidden behind a screen of riparian brush. At the Orchard picnic site, you'll pass a meadow planted with plums, walnuts, oaks, and a tot lot. Interpretive signs describe stream restoration efforts, the creatures (including California newts) that thrive among the redwoods, and other aspects of the unique environment.

Cross a bridge to the west side of the stream, pass through Fern Dell, and enter the first significant redwood grove of the hike, the Aurelia Henry Reinhardt Redwood Grove. From here on out you travel through the trees, with sunlight filtered through the dense canopy high overhead and the stream flowing in a needle-lined bed to the right (east). Picnic grounds line the stream side of the route.

The pavement ends at Trail's End, the end of the line for cyclists. The forest gets even quieter beyond, so quiet that banana slugs feel safe hanging out in the middle of the route. An occasional bench offers hikers the opportunity to sit and enjoy the absolute calm, and a chance to observe the ferns and bays that find purchase below the big trees.

The Stream Trail meets the Mill Trail at a bridge at the 1.5-mile mark; you'll find a picnic area in the broken sunshine on the east side of the bridge. When you've rested, return as you came to the trailhead.

Miles and Directions

0.0 Start.

0.2 Reach the Orchard picnic area. You've already passed through the Quail and Owl picnic sites; the first stretch of trail passes through one picnic ground after another, with the stream on the left (west).

0.3 Cross a bridge to the intersection with the West Ridge and Bridle Trails at Fern Dell. A shelter stands in the meadow to the left (west). Stay right (north) on the paved Stream Trail.

0.4 Pass through the Aurelia Henry Reinhardt Redwood Grove.

0.5 Pass the Old Church picnic area, with restrooms. A social trail climbs the canyon wall to the left (west); stay straight on the paved Stream Trail, passing Big Bend Meadow. Another social trail branches off to the right (east), dropping toward the creek and circling through a clearing before rejoining the main route.

0.8 The pavement ends at Trail's End, where the Stream Trail and the Bridle Trail meet in a clearing. There are restrooms, hitching posts, water, and a bike rack in the picnic area. Again, stay straight (north) on the wide, obvious Stream Trail.

1.0 Pass an interpretive sign.

1.3 Arrive at the intersection of the Fern and Stream Trails. Picnic tables, mossy stone barbecues, and water are available here. Stay straight (north) on the Stream Trail.

1.5 Reach the junction of the Stream and Mill Trails. This is the turnaround spot; you'll find restrooms (out of order in late 2008) and picnic tables across the bridge at the old mill site. Take a break streamside, then return as you came.

3.0 Return to the trailhead and parking area.

13 Grass Valley/Brandon Trail Loop (Anthony Chabot Regional Park)

Arguably the premier complex of public lands in this part of the East Bay, the adjoining Anthony Chabot and Lake Chabot parks see plenty of use. This loop takes you into a more remote part of Anthony Chabot Regional Park, where you'll enjoy a gentle tour of the rangeland and woodlands along Grass Valley Creek.

Distance: 3.4-mile loop.
Approximate hiking time: 2 hours.
Difficulty: Moderate due only to length.
Trail surface: Mostly dirt roadway, a short patch of paved road, optional dirt singletrack. Winter rains make the trail surface gloppy; park staff recommends hikers wait for a few days of dry weather before setting out.
Best season: Year-round.
Other trail users: Cyclists, equestrians, trail runners, cattle.
Canine compatibility: Leashed dogs permitted. Dogs may run off-leash outside of developed areas such as parking lots and picnic areas, but this is not recommended given that the trail is

shared with cyclists.
Fees and permits: None. You may be charged a $2 dog fee if you visit other areas of the parks.
Schedule: The parks are open from 7:00 a.m. to 10:00 p.m. daily.
Maps: USGS Oakland East and Las Trampas Ridge; East Bay Regional Park District brochure and map available at the trailhead and at www.ebparks.org.
Trail contact: East Bay Regional Park District, 2950 Peralta Oaks Court/P.O. Box 5381, Oakland, CA 94605-0381; (888) EBPARKS; www.ebparks.org.
Special considerations: No facilities are available at the trailhead. Bring drinking water with you. Do not leave valuables in your car;

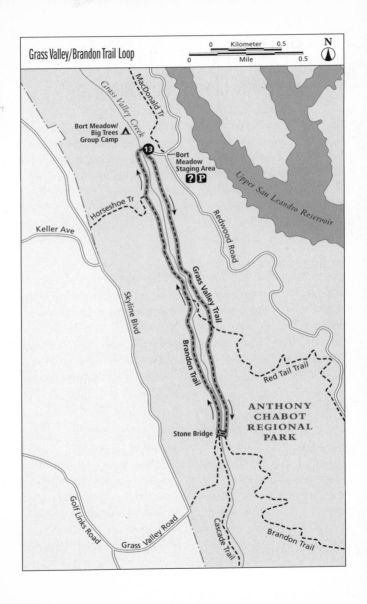

Grass Valley/Brandon Trail Loop

Kilometer 0 — 0.5
Mile 0 — 0.5

N

Grass Valley Creek
MacDonald Tr
Bort Meadow/
Big Trees
Group Camp
13
Bort
Meadow
Staging Area
? P
Upper San Leandro Reservoir
Horseshoe Tr
Keller Ave
Redwood Road
Grass Valley Trail
Skyline Blvd
Brandon Trail
Red Tail Trail
ANTHONY
CHABOT
REGIONAL
PARK
Stone Bridge
Golf Links Road
Grass Valley Road
Cascade Trail
Brandon Trail

the lot has been hit by what park staff calls "intermittent" thieves. **Other:** Cattle graze in Grass Valley's meadows. They are placid, but you'll have to make your way around them if they are on the trail.

Finding the trailhead: To reach the trailhead from Interstate 580 in the Castro Valley, take the Redwood Road exit. Head north on Redwood Road and follow it for about 10.5 miles to the Bort Meadow Staging Area, which is on the right (east) side of the winding park road. The trailhead is off the road to the left at the gated entrance to Skyline Trail/Grass Valley Road. *DeLorme Northern California Atlas & Gazetteer:* Page 105 C4. GPS: N37 46.660' W122 07.523'.

The Hike

Oh, Chabot. So much to do, so much to see. You can hike, swim, fish, camp, shoot, golf, and take boat tours. But ultimately, you can hike.

The Grass Valley and Brandon Trails are part of Anthony Chabot Regional Park, which abuts Lake Chabot Regional Park. Both parks are named for Anthony Chabot, an enterprising nineteenth-century businessman who, among other endeavors, built the dam that created the Lake Chabot reservoir in the 1870s. Portions of the parks were also, at one time, part of the colonial rancho system.

The trails travel through a shallow valley far removed from development and activity around Lake Chabot. Passing through a riparian habitat that on one side includes nonnative eucalyptus and on the other native oaks and bay laurels, the route is a pleasant pastoral escape.

The loop can be traveled in either direction; here it is described clockwise, beginning on the Grass Valley Trail and ending on the Brandon Trail. Both are former ranch roads, easy to follow and laid on easy grades alongside Grass Valley Creek.

You'll start by traveling down the paved and gated Grass Valley Road to the Grass Valley Trail itself. Pass through a cattle gate and head downhill through grazed meadowland on the sunny west-facing hillside east of the creek. A singletrack traces the roadway through the bed of the valley. You'll share the route with cows and their fragrant deposits, so watch your step.

About a mile down the trail, the landscape transitions from rangeland to eucalyptus forest. The spice of nonnative gum trees and occasional pines replaces the smell of sage, dry grass, and cow plops. A gate restricts the passage of cattle, and just beyond that you'll cross the stone bridge that spans Grass Valley Creek and leads to the Brandon Trail on the west side of the waterway. The creek is dry by late summer and in the fall, but flows through winter and spring.

Brandon Trail travels along the shady east-facing bank of the creek, through a more native riparian habitat of oaks, bay laurels, berries, and ferns—and a few stately redwoods. Cow pies have been replaced by horse cupcakes; you'll need to watch your step here as well. The trail climbs as gently as the Grass Valley Trail descended, nothing intimidating.

As you follow the Brandon Trail out of the narrower portion of the creek drainage and into the broader valley, you'll pass the Red Tail Trail. Between the Red Tail and Horseshoe Trails oak woodland and chaparral crowds the trail's edges. At the end of the loop the route passes a fire gate and curves through a clearing back to the paved Grass Valley Road. A short, steep climb up the pavement leads back to the trailhead.

Miles and Directions

0.0 Start by descending from the parking area down the gated, paved Grass Valley Road.

0.1 The Grass Valley Trail takes off from the paved road to the left (south).

0.8 The singletrack that has paralleled the broader Grass Valley Trail rises to meet the main route on the right (west).

0.9 Pass through an open gate and continue downhill on the road/trail. The meadow is slowly being left behind, with riparian habitat encroaching and old eucalyptus providing occasional shade.

1.1 Meet the Red Tail Trail on the left (east). Stay straight (south) on the Grass Valley Trail.

1.6 Pass through a gate and continue through a eucalyptus forest.

1.7 Arrive at the junction with the Brandon Trail. The stone bridge spanning Grass Valley Creek is to the right (west). Cross the bridge and turn right (north) on the Brandon Trail.

2.4 Pass the Red Tail Trail intersection, which leads right (east) toward the Grass Valley Trail and beyond. Stay straight (north) on the broad Brandon Trail.

3.0 The Horseshoe Trail heads left (west and uphill). Stay straight (north) on the Brandon Trail toward Bort Meadow.

3.2 Skirt a fire road gate and curve to the right (east) into a clearing. Merge right (east) onto the paved Grass Valley Road; another trail branches north toward Bort Meadow. Climb past the start of the loop at the Grass Valley Trail.

3.4 Reach the top of the hill and the trailhead and parking area.

14 Hayward Shoreline Loop (Hayward Regional Shoreline)

Narrow levees and scenic bridges support an amazing trail system that explores restored saltwater and freshwater marshes on the Hayward shoreline. Panoramic views open westward across the bay waters to San Francisco.

Distance: 3.5 miles of interlocking loops.
Approximate hiking time: 2 hours.
Difficulty: Moderate due only to length.
Trail surface: Dirt roadway, singletrack, wooden bridges, and two brief patches of pavement.
Best season: Year-round.
Other trail users: Cyclists, trail runners, bird-watchers.
Canine compatibility: No dogs permitted. Leashed dogs are allowed on the San Lorenzo Trail heading north from the Winton Avenue Staging Area.
Fees and permits: None.
Schedule: The park opens at 8:00 a.m. Gates are closed at 5:00 p.m., but you can park outside the gate on West Winton Avenue, where a trailhead permits access to the shoreline.

A curfew is imposed between 10:00 p.m. and 5:00 a.m.
Maps: USGS San Leandro; East Bay Regional Park District brochure and map available at the trailhead and at www.ebparks.org.
Trail contact: East Bay Regional Park District, 2950 Peralta Oaks Court/P.O. Box 5381, Oakland, CA 94605-0381; (888) EBPARKS; www.ebparks.org.
Special considerations: The trail is exposed to the vagaries of waterside weather. Be prepared for unimpeded wind, fog, and sun. Much of the Cogswell Marsh is under water at high tide but you'll stay high and dry on the levees.
Other: You'll find an information sign, trail maps, and a restroom at the trailhead, but no other amenities. Bring binoculars, a camera, and a key to identify birds.

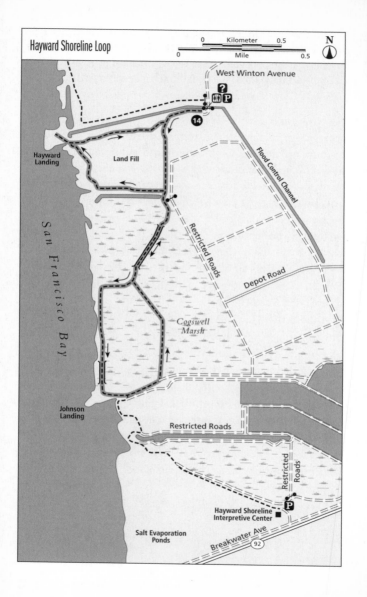

Hayward Shoreline Loop

0   Kilometer   0.5

0   Mile   0.5

N

West Winton Avenue

14

Hayward Landing

Land Fill

San Francisco Bay

Flood Control Channel

Restricted Roads

Depot Road

Cogswell Marsh

Johnson Landing

Restricted Roads

Restricted Roads

Hayward Shoreline Interpretive Center

Salt Evaporation Ponds

Breakwater Ave

92

Finding the trailhead: From Interstate 880 in Hayward, take the West Winton Avenue exit. Head west on Winton Avenue for 2.7 miles to its end at the park gate. There is plenty of parking at the trailhead. *DeLorme Northern California Atlas and Gazetteer:* Page 105 C4. GPS: N37 38.776' W122 08.845'.

The Hike

In the mid-1800s, the pristine marshlands along the east shore of San Francisco Bay were placed into production. Levees were erected to create salt evaporation ponds—the first in the Bay Area—producing a commodity that was highly valued as a preservative for food and was also used by miners in their labors.

It's an industry that became commonplace in the East and South Bays, and many of these ponds remain today, contained in an extensive patchwork of levees that's best appreciated from the air.

But at the Hayward Regional Shoreline, a marsh reclamation project has been underway for decades. Cogswell Marsh, which is circumnavigated as part of this hike, was the first pond reclaimed in 1980, and today no sign of saltworks remain—other than the levees, of course. Instead you'll see marsh plants such as the spindly, copper-tinged pickleweed, and shorebirds as plentiful as the waves lapping on the levee walls. Cogswell's 400-acre saltwater marsh supports more than ninety species, but the shoreline park also includes freshwater and brackish water marshland. Restoration efforts continue today.

The trail also links Johnson and Hayward Landings, which once were used to accommodate ferry and industrial traffic between the East Bay and San Francisco. On a clear day, the city's distinctive skyline will draw your gaze away from the shorebirds time and time again.

Just beyond the trailhead gate the Marsh Trail leads left (south) toward Cogswell Marsh. A salt evaporation pond and some industrial buildings are on the left (east), and the hummock of the landfill guards the bayside. Where the landfill ends the marsh begins, and you'll see views of San Francisco and the peninsula. Follow the levee out to the bridge that spans the tidal inlet of the marsh; the bay waters flow camouflage green and opaque below the wooden deck.

On the south side of the bridge the trail forks, forming a loop. You can go in either direction, but for the purposes of this description head right (west) to the outermost levee. Where the levee turns sharply south you'll find a viewing bench. Riprap protects the levee from the constant tickling of the waves, and allows small sandy beaches to build in its curves.

A second bridge spans the inlet of this section of the marsh. On the far side you'll arrive at Johnson Landing, a spit of land barely above water at high tide. From the landing the trail curves east, passing the trail link to the Hayward Shoreline Interpretive Center on the right (south). It then arcs north, following the levee to the first bridge.

Back at the trail junction with the landfill trail loop, turn left (west) and follow the landfill trail out to the water's edge. The track turns north at land's end, and continues to a concrete bridge spanning a flood control channel. Cross the bridge and walk out onto Hayward Landing, where again you can enjoy views across the bay to the silvery city on the horizon.

To return to the trailhead, cross back over the flood control channel and head east on the path adjacent to the landfill. This short stretch, abundant with birdlife and bird-watchers, leads to the parking lot and trailhead.

Miles and Directions

0.0   Start.

0.1   Turn left (south) on the Marsh Trail. Ignore side trails that lead onto the landfill, staying straight on the broad gravel road.

0.4   Reach the junction of the Marsh Trail and the trail that circles the landfill. Stay straight (south) on the Marsh Trail, passing a gated roadway and an interpretive sign that describes the Cogswell Marsh.

0.7   Arrive at the bridge that spans the inlet to the marsh. The trail splits on the far side. Head right (west) toward the outermost levee.

1.2   Reach the bridge over the second marsh inlet.

1.3   Pass Johnson Landing, an arcing spit of eroding mud and rocks. The trail turns inland (east).

1.5   At the junction with the trail that heads right (south) toward the Hayward Shoreline Interpretive Center, stay straight (east) on the Marsh Trail.

1.6   The trail turns north at a gate and an interpretive sign describing the endangered California least tern. The East Bay hills and Mount Diablo rise to the east.

2.0   Close the trail loop at the bridge spanning the Cogswell Marsh inlet.

2.5   On the far side of the bridge, turn left (west) and head out toward the bay on the trail that circles the landfill.

2.7   Pass a trail that heads right (north) across the front of the landfill, continuing west to a bench overlooking the bay. Turn right (north) at this point, following the waterfront.

3.0   Arrive at a trail junction at a concrete bridge that spans a flood control canal. Cross the bridge and go left (west) onto

Hayward Landing. A trail leads north from here through the Oro Loma Marsh to the park's Grant Avenue Staging Area. To complete the loop, cross back over the flood control channel and turn left (east) on the path back to the trailhead.

3.3   A trail marker directs you to the south side of the canal. Go right, then quickly left onto the wide dirt road.

3.5   Arrive back at the trailhead and parking area.

15 Dry Creek Trail Loop (Garin/Dry Creek Pioneer Regional Parks)

The heart of this park lies in its playing green, sycamore-shaded picnic areas, and at Jordan Pond. The Dry Creek Trail Loop ushers hikers away from that activity into a shady, secluded canyon, then climbs onto a ridge for quiet views across the bay.

Distance: 2.2-mile loop.

Approximate hiking time: 1.5 hours.

Difficulty: More challenging due to distance, elevation gain, and some tricky route finding.

Trail surface: Paved path, dirt road, dirt singletrack.

Best season: Spring and fall. The loop can be hiked year-round, but winter rains may render trail surfaces muddy.

Other trail users: Equestrians, trail runners, cyclists on portions of the trail around Jordan Pond and on the High Ridge Loop Trail.

Canine compatibility: Leashed dogs permitted.

Fees and permits: Entrance fee is $5 per car. The dog fee is $2.

Schedule: The park opens at 8:00 a.m. Specific closing times are posted at the entry kiosk. A curfew is imposed between 10:00 p.m. and 5:00 a.m.

Maps: USGS Niles and Newark; East Bay Regional Park District brochure and map available at the trailhead and at www .ebparks.org.

Trail contact: East Bay Regional Park District, 2950 Peralta Oaks Court/P.O. Box 5381, Oakland, CA 94605-0381; (888) EBPARKS; www.ebparks.org.

Special considerations: The park is home to rattlesnakes and mountain lions. While an encounter is unlikely, caution and common sense are advised. Bring a map on the trail; it can help clarify any confusion about route finding in the Dry Creek drainage.

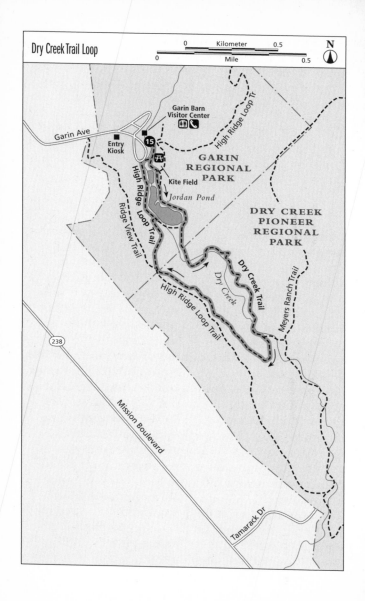

Dry Creek Trail Loop

| 0 | Kilometer | 0.5 |

| 0 | Mile | 0.5 |

N

Garin Ave

Entry Kiosk

15

Garin Barn
Visitor Center

High Ridge Loop Tr

GARIN
REGIONAL
PARK

Kite Field

Jordan Pond

DRY CREEK
PIONEER
REGIONAL
PARK

High Ridge Loop Trail

Ridge View Trail

High Ridge Loop Trail

Dry Creek

Dry Creek Trail

Meyers Ranch Trail

238

Mission Boulevard

Tamarack Dr

Other: Restrooms and water are available in the trailhead picnic areas and at the Garin Barn Visitor Center, which is open from 10:00 a.m. to 4:30 p.m. on weekends between Memorial Day and Labor Day. Fishing is permitted at Jordan Pond but no swimming is allowed.

Finding the trailhead: From Interstate 880 in Hayward, take the Whipple Road/Industrial Parkway exit. Head northeast on Industrial Parkway for 2 miles to Mission Boulevard (Highway 238). Go right (south) on Mission Boulevard for 0.1 mile to Garin Avenue. Turn left onto Garin Avenue and follow it 0.8 mile east to the park entry kiosk. Park in any of the lots and cross a bridge to the picnic area. Go south on the gravel path to the trailhead at the south end of the picnic green. *DeLorme Northern California Atlas and Gazetteer:* Page 105 C5. GPS: N37 37.604' W122 01.681'.

The Hike

You'll get lost on the Dry Creek Trail . . . but not really. Though route finding can be challenging as social trails intertwine in the Dry Creek drainage, it's more the lack of human traffic and signs of civilization that lend the route an air of seclusion.

The loop begins on the edge of the park's developed area. Once a working ranch, the park has a long history of hosting festive gatherings of family and friends. Its previous life as a ranch and farm is also in evidence near the trailhead, in the old barn that serves as a visitor center, the rusting farm machinery scattered on the grounds, and in the old apple orchard, which boasts about 200 trees and nearly that many varieties of "antique" apples. The apples are celebrated annually at the Garin Apple Festival; check the park's Web site for details.

The route starts at the southern edge of the large picnic green, dropping along Dry Creek (true to its name, running dry in summer and fall) to Jordan Pond. Families cluster around picnic tables shaded by willow and sycamore on the pond's shoreline and fish off the small pier. The pond is stocked with catfish and also supports a breeding population of bluegill and bass.

At the pond's earthen dam a trail marker points the way down the Dry Creek Trail. It's insta-nature at the dam's base: The track turns to dirt, birdcalls ring in the thick riparian brush bordering the banks, and old oaks and sycamores tangle overhead. You'll encounter the first unsigned trail forks not far from the dam: In most cases the braided trails link again, and if you are following the creek drainage, you are basically on course. In this instance take the left-hand track to one of several scenic bridges spanning the creek bed—the wooden structure is barely wide enough for a single person to pass.

Ignoring social trails that drop from the main track to the creek, proceed through a woodland so quiet you can hear lizards scrabbling in the leaf litter on the forest floor. Occasionally the distant holler of a train wafts into the canyon. Reach an interpretive post and an unmarked trail intersection at 0.6 mile and go right (south) to cross a second narrow wooden bridge. The path then climbs onto a hillside above the creek and traverses grassy slopes that host wildflowers in spring.

Take the middle track when the trail splits into three fingers, and drop through the dry creek bed. Climb to another unmarked trail intersection; a left turn takes you to the first sign of civilization since the bridge crossings—the marked junction of the Dry Creek and Old Ranch Trails. (Old Ranch Trail connects to Meyers Ranch Trail.)

Broad steps of timber and dirt reach up into an oak woodland that eventually gives way to grassland. Pass through a gate and follow the singletrack trail just below the High Ridge Loop Trail, where views open across the Dry Creek valley to the eastern hills. At the junction with the Ridge View Trail the track finally tops the ridge crest; take a break on the bench at the trail junction and enjoy the views across the sprawling East Bay. A short descent drops you on the western shoreline of Jordan Pond. The picnic areas and parking lots are just north of the pond.

Miles and Directions

0.0 Start.

0.2 Circle Jordan Pond to the Dry Creek Trail sign and head down the paved path to the base of the dam, where the trail surface changes to dirt. Though off-limits to bikes, keep an eye open as wheel tracks in the dirt indicate cyclists poach the trail.

0.3 The trail splits; stay left (east). You can take the right-hand trail as well; it rejoins the main route on the far side of the bridge.

0.5 Cross the one-person bridge that spans the creek.

0.6 At the unmarked trail intersection stay right (southwest).

0.7 Cross another singletrack bridge. At the junction on the far side, go right; the left-hand trail circles back to meet the main trail in a little loop.

1.0 After traversing a hillside above the creek, the trail splits into three tracks. Take the middle track, and drop down across the dry creek bed. Climb past trail marker 9 to an unmarked trail intersection and go left (south).

1.1 Arrive at the signed intersection of the Dry Creek Trail and the Old Ranch Trail. Turn right (southwest) on the Dry Creek Trail.

1.2 Climb a broad timber-and-dirt staircase to an unsigned trail intersection. Turn right (northwest) and follow the path that climbs along the east side of the fence.

1.5 Pass through a gate and follow the singletrack trail just below the High Ridge Loop Trail, traversing hillsides below the crest of the ridge.

1.8 Pass several interpretive markers and a cluster of lovely buckeye trees to the junction with the Ridge View Trail. A bench offers amazing views west across the bay. Go right (north) through the gate onto the High Ridge Loop Trail (also signed FIRE ROAD 11A).

2.0 The High Ridge Loop Trail drops quickly to the west shore of Jordan Pond. Turn left (north) and follow the pond road toward the picnic green and visitor center.

2.2 Arrive back at the trailhead on the picnic green.

16 Bayview Trail (Coyote Hills Regional Park)

For hundreds of years the Coyote Hills formation met all the needs of the native peoples who lived here. These days, with views reaching west across San Francisco Bay, raptors wheeling overhead, and shorebirds feasting in the marshlands, trails in the hills nourish the spirit of every hiker who visits.

Distance: 3-mile loop.
Approximate hiking time: 1.5 hours.
Difficulty: Moderate due only to length.
Trail surface: Pavement, dirt road.
Best season: Spring for wildflowers and fall for the best weather, but the trail can be hiked year-round.
Other trail users: Cyclists, bird-watchers, trail runners.
Canine compatibility: Leashed dogs permitted.
Fees and permits: A $5 per car fee is levied. The dog fee is $2.
Schedule: The park opens at 8:00 a.m. daily; specific closing hours are posted at the entry kiosk. A curfew is imposed between 10:00 p.m. and 5:00 a.m.

Maps: USGS Newark; East Bay Regional Park District brochure and map available at the trail-head and at www.ebparks.org.
Trail contact: East Bay Regional Park District, 2950 Peralta Oaks Court/P.O. Box 5381, Oakland, CA 94605-0381; (888) EBPARKS; www.ebparks.org.
Special considerations: You'll find water, restrooms, and picnic facilities at the trailhead. Please don't disturb or collect archaeological artifacts in the park.
Other: The park's visitor center is home to extensive interpretive information and displays of native Ohlone culture. Exhibits include descriptions of basket-weaving techniques, a tule canoe, and an exquisite mural depicting life in the hills before

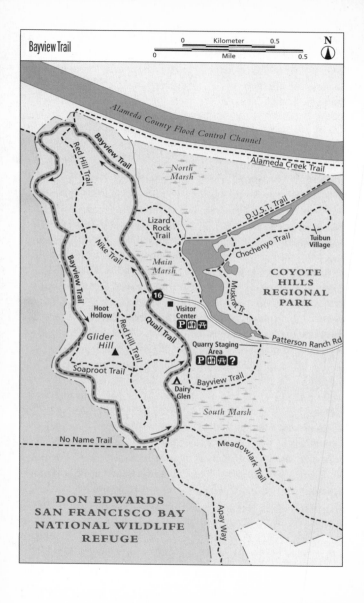

Bayview Trail

0   Kilometer   0.5

0   Mile   0.5

N

Alameda County Flood Control Channel

Alameda Creek Trail

Bayview Trail

Red Hill Trail

North
Marsh

D.U.S.T. Trail

Lizard
Rock
Trail

Chochenyo Trail

Tuibun
Village

Nike Trail

Main
Marsh

COYOTE
HILLS
REGIONAL
PARK

Bayview Trail

Muskrat Tr

16

Hoot
Hollow

Visitor
Center

P

Glider
Hill

Red Hill Trail

Quail Trail

Quarry Staging
Area

P

?

Patterson Ranch Rd

Soaproot Trail

Bayview Trail

Dairy
Glen

No Name Trail

South Marsh

Meadowlark Trail

DON EDWARDS
SAN FRANCISCO BAY
NATIONAL WILDLIFE
REFUGE

Apay Way

the arrival of Europeans. The center is open from 9:30 a.m. to 5:00 p.m. Tuesday through Sunday, and is closed on Thanksgiving and Christmas. A nectar garden adjoins the visitor center, with penstemons, sages, milkweed, and other fragrant California native blossoms attracting butterflies year-round. Overnight camping is available to organized groups (not the general public) at the Dairy Glen site. Contact the EBRPD for further information and to make reservations.

Finding the trailhead: From Interstate 880 in Fremont, take the Alvarado/Fremont Boulevard North exit. Go southeast on Fremont Boulevard for 0.6 mile to Paseo Padre Parkway and turn right (west). Follow Paseo Padre Parkway for 2 miles to Patterson Ranch Road. Go right (northwest) on Patterson Ranch Road for 0.5 mile to the park entry, then proceed another 0.8 mile to the visitor center parking lot and trailhead. Alternatively, you can take the Highway 84/ Dumbarton Bridge exit from I-880. Take the Paseo Padre Parkway exit, turn right (north) on Paseo Padre Parkway, and go 1 mile to Patterson Ranch Road, which you'll follow to the park entrance and visitor center. *DeLorme Northern California Atlas and Gazetteer:* Page 105 D5. GPS: N37 33.252' W122 05.510'.

The Hike

Long home to the native Ohlone people, who once hunted game in the woodlands and fished along the bay shore, the Coyote Hills now provide modern visitors with a harvest of bountiful views and peace of mind.

Prefacing your hike with an exploration of Ohlone culture will promote greater appreciation for the richness of the marshlands and grasslands of the 978-acre park. The area's rich native heritage is described thoroughly in the visitor center—well worth a visit.

And then there are the birds. Ducks and egrets cluster

in the marshlands, shorebirds stalk the mudflats, songbirds flit through the grasses and oaks and raptors perch on high rocks watching, watching, watching for the unwary ground squirrel.

The Bayview Trail traverses the grasslands above the marsh and bay shore, providing the perfect venue for sight-seeing. It begins by spanning the flats between the main marsh and Glider Hill, a popular spot for radio-controlled airplanes. Grasslands predominate along the outset of the trail, thick with wildflowers in season. The hilltops are studded with rock formations, Red Hill on the left (west) and Lizard Rock on the right (east).

Pass junctions with the Nike Trail (named for the Nike missile installation that once operated in the hills) on the left (west) and paths that lead right (east) to Lizard Rock and the main marsh. Beyond a saddle views open north onto the Alameda Creek flood control channel and paved Alameda Creek Trail, a regional path that stretches 12 miles inland to Niles Canyon.

Those views are awesome, but the main event becomes apparent when you swing onto the west side of the park and traverse above the wave-puckered waters of San Francisco Bay. The bay and salt evaporation ponds just offshore are protected by the Don Edwards San Francisco Bay National Wildlife Refuge, and you'll likely catch sight of herons, egrets, gulls, ducks, and other birds wading at low tide or flying low over the green surface looking for a meal. In the distance the smoky Santa Cruz Mountains scrape the sky. Southward the Dumbarton Bridge spans the bay, reaching into the silvery development on the western shore.

Several trails offer options to hitch over the hills back to the east side of the park, but there's no need to leave the

Bayview Trail. It eventually curves inland through a gap to the border of the south marsh. Follow the trail above the Dairy Glen group camp to the junction with the Quail Trail, which climbs through another saddle and drops north to the visitor center and trailhead.

Miles and Directions

0.0 Start on the paved trail beyond the gate at the north end of the visitor center parking lot.

0.1 Pass the Nike Trail intersection. Stay straight (north) on the paved Bayview Trail.

0.3 Climb into a saddle, passing intersections with the Lizard Rock Trail on the right (east) and a social trail that leads left (west) to Red Hill.

0.7 Pass the intersection with the formal Red Hill Trail on the left (south). A separate trail drops right (north) to the Alameda Creek Trail. Stay straight (west) on the Bayview Trail.

0.8 Reach a viewing platform and a side trail to the little beach and levee below. Stay left (south) on the Bayview Trail.

1.3 Pass the western endpoint of the Nike Trail on the left (east) and continue straight (south) on the Bayview Trail.

1.7 Reach the junction with the Soaproot Trail, which climbs to the left (southeast), over the hilltop and back to the visitor center. Continue straight (south) on the Bayview Trail.

2.4 A gentle traversing climb leads around the southern knees of the hills and east toward the South Marsh, where you'll intersect the No Name Trail and Apay Way. Remain on the paved Bayview Trail.

2.5 Reach the junction with the Meadowlark Trail on the right (south). Stay left (east) on the Bayview Trail, which climbs around the Dairy Glen group camp and offers views eastward to Mission and Monument Peaks.

2.7 Arrive at the junction of the Soaproot, Bayview, and Quail

Trails. Head left (up and north) on the Quail Trail, a broad dirt track that climbs toward a saddle. Social trails depart right and left from the Quail Trail at its apex; stay straight on the roadway.

2.9 Head downhill past the Hoot Hollow picnic area. Continue straight (north) on the Quail Trail.

3.0 Pass the Glider Hill Trail as you descend to the picnic areas and lawns surrounding the visitor center, trailhead, and parking area.

17 Indian Joe Creek Trail to Cave Rocks (Sunol-Ohlone Regional Wilderness)

Climb alongside a seasonal stream to a dark jumble of basalt known as Cave Rocks, popular with climbers and a lovely vista point for views down the Indian Joe Creek drainage.

Distance: 2.8 miles out and back.

Approximate hiking time: 2 hours.

Difficulty: More challenging due to a steady, sometimes steep climb and descent.

Trail surface: Dirt road, dirt singletrack.

Best season: Spring and late fall. The trail can be hiked year-round, but can be very hot in late summer and muddy after a rainstorm.

Other trail users: Trail runners.

Canine compatibility: Leashed dogs permitted.

Fees and permits: A $5 per car fee is levied. The dog fee is $2.

Schedule: The park opens at 8:00 a.m. daily. Closing hours are posted at the entry kiosk. A curfew is imposed between 10:00 p.m. and 5:00 a.m.

Maps: USGS La Costa Valley;

East Bay Regional Park District brochure and map available at the trailhead and at www.ebparks.org.

Trail contact: East Bay Regional Park District, 2950 Peralta Oaks Court/P.O. Box 5381, Oakland, CA 94605-0381; (888) EBPARKS; www.ebparks.org.

Special considerations: No potable water is available in the park, so be sure to bring drinking water. Use restrooms at the trailhead. The park is home to rattlesnakes and mountain lions. While an encounter is unlikely, caution and common sense are advised.

Other: Inside the charming Old Green Barn Interpretive Center you'll find various historical and ecological displays, including terrariums housing different varieties of snakes found in the park. You can also pick up an

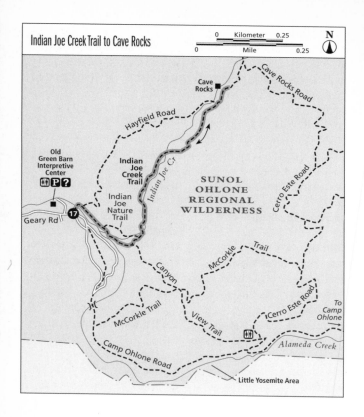

Indian Joe Creek Trail to Cave Rocks

0 Kilometer 0.25
0 Mile 0.25

N

Cave Rocks
Cave Rocks Road
Hayfield Road
Old Green Barn Interpretive Center
Indian Joe Creek Trail
Indian Joe Cr
Indian Joe Nature Trail
Geary Rd
17
SUNOL OHLONE REGIONAL WILDERNESS
Cerro Este Road
Canyon
McCorkle Trail
McCorkle Trail
View Trail
Cerro Este Road
To Camp Ohlone
Camp Ohlone Road
Alameda Creek
Little Yosemite Area

interpretive guide to the Indian Joe Nature Trail. Keys to identification of the birds, butterflies, and wildflowers are available here as well. Sunol-Ohlone Regional Wilderness offers overnight camping and backpacking options by reservation. Obtain a permit in advance by contacting the park via telephone or online. Trailhead facilities include restrooms, doggie waste-disposal bags, picnic tables, and trash receptacles.

Finding the trailhead: To reach the trailhead from Interstate 680 in Sunol, take the Highway 84 exit. Calaveras Road, which heads south to the park, departs from the east side of the interchange, opposite Paloma Road into Sunol. Follow Calaveras Road 4.1 miles south to Geary Road. Turn left (east) on Geary Road and follow it for 0.8 mile to the park boundary, then for another mile to the entry kiosk and parking areas (1.8 miles total). The trailhead is adjacent to the visitor center, which is served by the parking lot to the north (left) of the entry kiosk. *DeLorme Northern California Atlas and Gazetteer:* Page 105 D7. GPS: N37 30.964' W121 49.899'.

The Hike

The obvious apex of this hike is Cave Rocks, a basalt formation that overlooks Indian Joe Creek and is sometimes hung with the ropes of rock climbers honing their skills on the polished surfaces. The rocks are tipped and balanced, creating dark alcoves that lend truth to the tale told by a park ranger—that a native named Indian Joe once lived near here.

Indian Joe, according to a park brochure, was a native who worked for homesteaders Pat and Mary Ann Geary. The Gearys purchased this section of untamed land from the U.S. government after the end of the Civil War and built a cabin next to Indian Joe Creek. Later generations built the Old Green Barn (1895) and other structures on the property, including the one-room Rosedale School, which saw the education of two generations of Gearys and other area residents before being torn down in 1918. The property was acquired as open space in 1959.

The route begins alongside Alameda Creek on the combined Indian Joe Nature/Canyon View/Ohlone Wilderness Trails. The creek runs all year, watering a healthy riparian zone of oaks, willows, and sycamores.

Leave one creek drainage for a smaller, seasonal stream when you turn north onto the Indian Joe Creek Trail, which rollercoasters to the junction with the Canyon View Trail. Stay left at this juncture, dropping into the Indian Joe Creek valley. Close the gate behind you, and the mostly shady trek upstream to Cave Rocks commences.

The route crosses the creek a number of times in the lower canyon, circumnavigating stately oaks and white-barked sycamores. One crossing leads under the spider-arm branches of a fallen oak, vaguely creepy but very cool—and quite likely ephemeral, as time, water, and rot are sure to wear the wood away. You'll be an expert at rock hopping (in the wet season) in no time; in summer the creek cobbles are dry and present no more challenge to your passage than a divot on a golf course.

After an easy mile the trail begins to climb in earnest, switchbacking onto the hill on the east side of Indian Joe Creek. The ascent is steady, with views opening down valley (south) and up to the ridgetops ahead (north). Oaks pepper the grasslands, offering shade between steep grassy pitches.

The trail moderates in a clearing shaded by a grand old oak and passes the upper end of Hayfield Road. The rocks are a short climb above, on the left (west) side of the trail.

Take some time to explore the rocks, polished to an almost glassy finish on some surfaces and painted with orange lichen and climbers' chalk on others. Social trails lead into the alcoves and up to the top of the formation, where vistas down Indian Joe Creek spread out and away. Enjoy the views then return as you came.

Miles and Directions

0.0 Start to the right (east) of the Old Green Barn, walking behind the park residence and adjacent picnic grounds to a bridge spanning Alameda Creek.

0.1 On the north side of the bridge turn right (east) on the combined Indian Joe Nature/Canyon View/Ohlone Wilderness Trails. The track leads past the Hayfield Road intersection and several interpretive markers.

0.3 Pass a side trail and cross a seasonal stream before you reach a trail junction. Go left (up and north) on the Indian Joe Creek and Indian Joe Nature Trails.

0.5 Reach the Canyon View Trail junction and stay left (north) on the Indian Joe Nature Trail. The path narrows to singletrack and drops into the Indian Joe Creek drainage. At the trail marker the Indian Joe Creek and Indian Joe Nature Trails split. Head right (north), through the gate, on the Indian Joe Creek Trail.

0.9 After negotiating a number of stream crossings, the trail switchbacks up and away from the creek.

1.3 Climb through oak-studded grasslands to the junction with Hayfield Road. Stay straight (north) on the Indian Joe Creek Trail.

1.4 Arrive at Cave Rocks. Scramble about (or climb if you are trained), take in the views, then return as you came.

2.8 Arrive back at the trailhead.

18 Canyon View Trail and Camp Ohlone Road (Sunol-Ohlone Regional Wilderness)

The Canyon View Trail offers just that—views down into an Alameda Creek gorge dubbed Little Yosemite. Steep walls and the jostling stream enliven the stretch of Camp Ohlone Road that traverses the canyon floor.

Distance: 3.3-mile loop.

Approximate hiking time: 2 hours.

Difficulty: More challenging due to distance and a relatively steep ascent on the Canyon View Trail.

Trail surface: Dirt and gravel roads, dirt singletrack.

Best season: Spring and late fall. The trail can be hiked year-round, but can be very hot in late summer and muddy after a rainstorm.

Other trail users: Equestrians, backpackers, trail runners, the occasional automobile on Camp Ohlone Road, and cattle.

Canine compatibility: Leashed dogs permitted.

Fees and permits: A $5 per car fee is levied. The dog fee is $2.

Schedule: The park opens at 8:00 a.m. daily. Closing hours are posted at the entry kiosk. A curfew is imposed between 10:00 p.m. and 5:00 a.m.

Maps: USGS La Costa Valley; East Bay Regional Park District brochure and map available at the trailhead and at www .ebparks.org.

Trail contact: East Bay Regional Park District, 2950 Peralta Oaks Court/P.O. Box 5381, Oakland, CA 94605-0381; (888) EBPARKS; www.ebparks.org.

Special considerations: No potable water is available in the park, so be sure to bring drinking water. The park is home to rattlesnakes and mountain lions. While an encounter is unlikely,

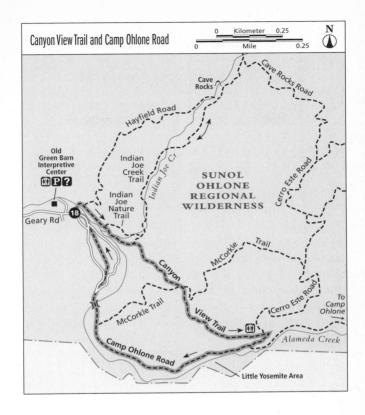

Canyon View Trail and Camp Ohlone Road

Kilometer 0 — 0.25
Mile 0 — 0.25

N

Cave Rocks Road

Cave Rocks

Hayfield Road

Old Green Barn Interpretive Center

Indian Joe Creek Trail

Indian Joe Nature Trail

Indian Joe Cr

SUNOL OHLONE REGIONAL WILDERNESS

Cerro Este Road

Geary Rd

18

Canyon

McCorkle Trail

View Trail

McCorkle Trail

Cerro Este Road

To Camp Ohlone

Camp Ohlone Road

Alameda Creek

Little Yosemite Area

caution and common sense are advised.

Other: Check out the Old Green Barn Interpretive Center, where you'll find various historical and ecological displays. Keys that will help you identify the birds, butterflies, and wildflowers are also available here. Sunol-Ohlone

Regional Wilderness offers overnight camping and backpacking options by reservation. Obtain permits in advance by contacting the park via telephone or online. Trailhead facilities include restrooms, doggie waste-disposal bags, picnic tables, and trash receptacles.

Finding the trailhead: To reach the trailhead from Interstate 680 in Sunol, take the Highway 84 exit. Calaveras Road, which heads south to the park, departs from the east side of the interchange, opposite Paloma Road into Sunol. Follow Calaveras Road 4.1 miles south to Geary Road. Turn left (east) on Geary Road and follow it for 0.8 mile to the park boundary, then for another mile to the entry kiosk and parking areas (1.8 miles total). The trailhead is adjacent to the visitor center, which is served by the parking lot to the north (left) of the entry kiosk. *DeLorme Northern California Atlas and Gazetteer:* Page 105 D7. GPS: N37 30.964' W121 49.899'.

The Hike

Birds and butterflies, wildflowers and archetypal oaks, serpentine rock outcrops painted with lichen and mossy creek boulders washed in a clear stream . . . this loop pretty much epitomizes the best of an easy Bay Area day hike.

It begins with a climb through Jacob's Valley, a picturesque grassland dotted with serpentine rock outcrops and perfectly shaped oaks, tops out with an easy traverse offering excellent views in three directions, and drops into Little Yosemite, a steep gorge containing boulder-tossed Alameda Creek.

This route passes through an area grazed by lumbering bovines, but don't let the cow pies dissuade you. Watch your step and enjoy.

You'll start out on the Indian Joe Nature Trail (same as for the Indian Joe Creek route). At the Indian Joe/Canyon View Trail split, head right (southeast) and uphill on the Canyon View Trail, passing through the gate and into Jacob's Valley.

Rustic fence lines, cropped grasses, and worn cattle tracks hearken back to the past; this land has been grazed for generations. But it's also rich in natural diversity, with wildflowers blooming until late summer and lizards scurrying off the trail and away from the hazards of hiking shoes. Oaks shade rock outcrops that sport black and green lichen outerwear.

Pass the McCorkle Trail intersection and the route begins a pleasant traverse across open grassy hills. Views open south, then east on a classic panorama of rolling hills and the steep upper walls of Little Yosemite. Railroad tie–sized timbers span a muddy cattle track below a water trough in the shade of a sycamore tree, then the trail descends to an overlook of the Little Yosemite area.

Continue downhill to the junction of the Canyon View Trail and Camp Ohlone Road in Little Yosemite. Side trails branch off the roadway to the creek, where you can enjoy the cascades. The steep dark valley walls overshadow the stream and its verdant riparian plant life.

Straightforward Camp Ohlone Road follows the creek back west, then north, to the more developed portions of the park. Any number of social paths lead down to the stream, but visitors are cautioned not to swim or wade. A lovely trussed bridge spans the creek at the Camp Ohlone Road trailhead; the last part of the loop follows an equestrian trail wedged between parking lots and picnic sites to the trailhead at the visitor center.

Miles and Directions

0.0   Start to the right (east) of the Old Green Barn, walking behind the park residence and adjacent picnic grounds to a bridge spanning Alameda Creek.

0.1   On the north side of the bridge, turn right (east) on the combined Indian Joe Nature/Canyon View/Ohlone Wilderness Trails. The flat, obvious track leads past Hayfield Road.

0.3   Pass a side trail and cross a seasonal stream before reaching a trail junction. Go left (up and north) on the combined Indian Joe Creek/Canyon View Trails.

0.5 The Canyon View Trail splits off right (southeast).

0.6 A steep ascent leads to a gate; close this after you pass. Continue climbing, with views opening down and right (west) to the valley floor.

0.7 Pass a trail marker for the Ohlone Wilderness Trail. Ignore side trails and continue uphill and southeast.

0.8 Reach the McCorkle Trail intersection on the left (east) and continue straight (southeast) on the Canyon View Trail.

1.0 Timbers bridge the cattle track to a sycamore-shaded water trough.

1.2 The trail arcs east onto the steep slopes above Little Yosemite. Hikers with vertigo be forewarned; the trail is exposed for a short distance before reaching a side trail that branches right (south) to an overlook.

1.3 Drop down either of the twin tracks to a gate and trail sign at the junction with the Cerro Este Road. Turn right (south) on the Canyon View Trail, skirting another water trough.

1.5 Arrive at the junction with Camp Ohlone Road, where you'll find picnic tables and a restroom. Turn right (west) on Camp Ohlone Road.

2.1 Pass a fence line and gate. A number of social trails drop left (south) to the creek; stay straight on Camp Ohlone Road.

2.4 Pass another fence line and gate.

2.7 Cross a scenic bridge constructed of heavy timbers that spans Alameda Creek. The trail is paved on the far side, leading past trailhead information and restrooms into a large parking area. Pick up the equestrian trail that traverses the field between the loop of the road.

3.1 The equestrian trail ends at the horse trailer parking lot. At the stop sign go left (north) on the paved park road toward the visitor center.

3.3 Arrive back at the visitor center, trailhead, and parking area.

19 Hidden Valley/Peak Meadow Trail Loop (Mission Peak Regional Preserve)

Dominating the ridgelines of the southernmost East Bay, even the easiest hikes on the steep exposed faces of Mission Peak pose a challenge. But spectacular views reward sweat and effort.

Distance: 3.7-mile lollipop.

Approximate hiking time: 2 to 3 hours.

Difficulty: More challenging due to steepness and distance.

Trail surface: Dirt roads and singletrack.

Best season: Year-round, but this can be a hot, exposed trudge in summertime heat. Late fall, clear winter days, and early spring offer the coolest hiking.

Other trail users: Mountain bikers, equestrians, trail runners, hang gliders, radio-controlled airplane operators.

Canine compatibility: Leashed dogs permitted.

Fees and permits: None.

Schedule: The park is open from 8:00 a.m. to sunset daily. A curfew is imposed between 10:00 p.m. and 5:00 a.m.

Maps: USGS Niles; East Bay Regional Park District brochure and map available at the trailhead and at www.ebparks.org.

Trail contact: East Bay Regional Park District, 2950 Peralta Oaks Court/P.O. Box 5381, Oakland, CA 94605-0381; (888) EBPARKS; www.ebparks.org.

Special considerations: The park is home to rattlesnakes and mountain lions. While an encounter is unlikely, caution and common sense are advised. Water is available at the trailhead but not along the trail. Bring plenty of water with you.

Hidden Valley/Peak Meadow Trail Loop

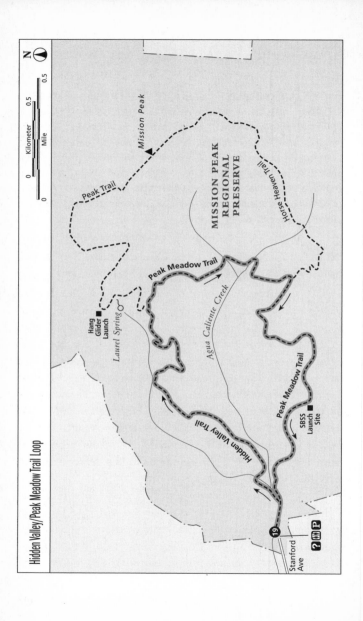

Other: Restrooms, picnic facilities, trash bins, an informational
billboard, and a bike rack are at
the trailhead.

Finding the trailhead: To reach the trailhead from Interstate 680
in Fremont, take the Mission Boulevard exit. Head south on Mission
Boulevard, passing historic Mission San Jose and Ohlone College, to
Stanford Avenue. Turn left (east) on Stanford Avenue and go 0.6 mile
to the park entrance. Limited parking is available in the trailhead lot,
which can fill quickly on weekends. Additional parking can be found
on nearby residential streets. The trailhead is at the east end of the
lot. *DeLorme Northern California Atlas & Gazetteer:* Page 105 D6.
GPS: N37 30.250' W121 54.478'.

The Hike

Without doubt this is the toughest trek in this guide.
Still, some hikers will think that because the route doesn't
include the summit it's a cop-out. With an elevation gain of
about 1,000 feet, I beg to differ.

As it is, the loop is at the outer limit of the easy cat-
egory. Those who question the strength of their knees,
hearts, or lungs should think twice before taking it on. But
for any fit hiker this is very doable, and you'll encounter
people of all ages and body shapes heading up and down
the mountain at the pace that suits them. You'll also be
treated to a symphony of languages, as fellow hikers hail
from a grab bag of distant lands including Europe, India,
Asia, and Africa.

They don't come to sweat—they come for the views.
Offering the best vistas in this part of the East Bay, the
west-facing slopes of Mission Peak overlook most of the
southern bay region, with rolling hills, patchwork suburbs,
flashing salt evaporation ponds, glittering bay waters, and

the dark summits of the Santa Cruz Mountains layered to the blue-sky horizon.

The climb begins immediately. Head up on the Hidden Valley Trail (also the Ohlone Wilderness Trail), passing the junction with Peak Meadow Trail, the return route, on the right (south). The ragged summit of Mission Peak, a wall of exposed and broken rock, rises above undulations of steep grassland. Pillows of green oaks huddle in gullies, sucking water from the ravines they shade. A wind sock flutters on the high hill, an indicator for hang gliders who come to the mountain to launch. To the south, broadcast antennae erupt from the summit of Mount Allison; Monument Peak is the next high point in the range.

The route is exposed, so you can follow the progress of other hikers on their ascents. Trails are not well signed (except for those that have been posted as closed), but the Hidden Valley track is wide and unmistakable; ignore social trails cut by thoughtless trekkers.

Viewing benches are positioned at overlooks along the trail, offering the opportunity to rest and take in the sights. You can use any of these benches as turnaround points; the first is at 0.7 mile, offering a 1.4-mile out-and-back adventure. Another is at the 1-mile mark, and yet another at 1.2 miles.

A rolling, scenic descent begins when you leave the Hidden Valley Trail on the Peak Meadow Trail. This less-used route traverses south across the mountainside, offering both views and a tree-shrouded passage through the upper reaches of the Agua Caliente Creek drainage. The habitat change is stark and abrupt, from sun-baked grassland to oak woodland nurtured by a creek that dives underground during the dry season.

From the junction with the Horse Heaven Trail at 2.4 miles, the downhill run becomes as steep as the uphill, a knee-pounding drop on a roadway cut into red earth. At the mountain's foot you'll reach a corral and merge with a ranch road, which climbs gently back to the trailhead.

Miles and Directions

0.0 Start.

0.1 At the intersection with the Peak Meadow Trail stay left (up and northeast) on the Hidden Valley/Ohlone Wilderness Trail.

0.4 Cross a cattle guard and keep up on either of the parallel trails. Pass a number of closed social trails; avoid using them as the exposed earth is prone to erosion.

0.7 Views of the South Bay open as the trail crests a shoulder of the mountain at a bench. Continue upward on the Hidden Valley Trail.

1.0 Pass a second bench and vista point. The social trail that departs left is closed. Keep up on the Hidden Valley Trail.

1.2 Switchback up to another bench. You'll find a trail marker and a trashcan here too.

1.4 Reach the start of the Peak Meadow Trail, denoted with a worn Ohlone Wilderness Trail signpost and a green fire department road post marked 4 16B. There is no Peak Meadow Trail sign. Turn right (south) on the narrower, less used dirt track.

1.6 Pass a water trough for livestock on the right (west).

2.1 A big leaf maple marks the start of the traverse through the Agua Caliente Creek drainage. For the next 0.2 mile you'll enjoy the shade of an oak woodland habitat.

2.4 Climb to the junction with the Horse Heaven Trail. Turn right (west and downhill) on the Peak Meadow Trail.

2.7 A spring burbles on the left side of the trail, supporting a patch of greenery through even the hottest part of the summer.

3.4 On the flatlands at the base of the mountain, merge with a ranch road and pass a gate.

3.6 Dip through a seasonal stream drainage, then merge with the Hidden Valley/Ohlone Wilderness Trail.

3.7 Retrace your steps to the trailhead.

Trail Index

About the Author

Tracy Salcedo-Chourré has written more than a dozen guidebooks to destinations in Colorado and California, including *Hiking Lassen Volcanic National Park, Exploring California's Missions and Presidios, Exploring Point Reyes National Seashore and the Golden Gate National Recreation Area, Best Rail-Trails California,* and *Best Easy Day Hikes* guides to the San Francisco Bay Area, Denver, Boulder, Aspen, and Lake Tahoe. She is also an editor, teacher, and soccer mom—and still finds time to hike, cycle, swim, and walk the dog. She lives with her husband, three sons, and small menagerie of pets in California's Wine Country.

You can learn more about her by visiting her Web page at the FalconGuide site, www.falcon.com/user/172. Her guidebooks are available online through Falcon/The Globe Pequot Press, at various outdoor shops, and through local and national booksellers.

WHAT'S SO SPECIAL ABOUT UNSPOILED, NATURAL PLACES?

Beauty   Solitude   Wildness   Freedom   Quiet   Adventure
Serenity   Inspiration   Wonder   Excitement
Relaxation   Challenge

There's a lot to love about our treasured public lands, and the reasons are different for each of us. Whatever your reasons are, the national **Leave No Trace** education program will help you discover special outdoor places, enjoy them, and preserve them—today and for those who follow. By practicing and passing along these simple principles, you can help protect the special places you love from being loved to death.

THE PRINCIPLES OF **LEAVE NO TRACE**

- Plan ahead and prepare
- Travel and camp on durable surfaces
- Dispose of waste properly
- Leave what you find
- Minimize campfire impacts
- Respect wildlife
- Be considerate of other visitors

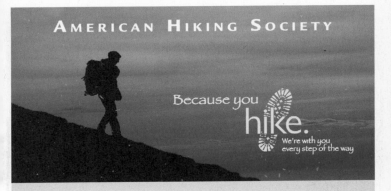